HOW TO BECOME JEWISH

(AND WHY NOT TO)

AN IMPRACTICAL GUIDE TO CONVERTING TO JUDAISM

BY DANIEL GREENBERG

Published by Daniel Greenberg Limited
9 Holders Hill Crescent, London NW4 1NE
dgreenberg@hotmail.co.uk
2009

© Daniel Greenberg 2009
All rights reserved and asserted (including the right to be identified as the author of this work) by Daniel Greenberg.
It is contrary to Jewish and secular law to copy any part of this book without the express permission of the author.

Dedicated with love and gratitude to all those who have allowed me to accompany them during any part of their inspiring and arduous journey

CONTENTS

Preface
Glossary of Hebrew Expressions
Question 1 – Why would anyone want to become Jewish?
Question 2 – How do "regularisation" cases arise?
Question 3 – How do "marriage" cases arise?
Question 4 – Why does anyone want to become a "real" convert?
Question 5 – What exactly is conversion?
Question 6 – How does the process work today in the United Kingdom?
Question 7 – How does the process work in America?
Question 8 – How does the process work in Israel?
Question 9 – What are the basic skills a candidate needs to master?
Question 10 – How much does conversion cost?
Question 11 – How long does the process take?
Question 12 – Will I need to be circumcised?

Question 13 – Which is the best country to convert in?
Question 14 – Which Beth Din should I choose?
Question 15 – Why should I have an orthodox conversion?
Question 16 – Is it really necessary to be so hard on prospective converts?
Question 17 – Why does Judaism not proselytise?
Question 18 – What status do converts have in the Jewish community?
Question 19 – So what does the convert get out of the process?
Question 20 – What kind of Jew should I become?
Question 21 – Need conversion cut me off from my family and friends?
Question 22 – Do I have to be a Zionist to become Jewish?
Question 23 – What most needs to be changed?
Afterthought

PREFACE

This book is nominally a short guide to the process of converting to Judaism. It could therefore profitably be read by anyone who has formed a curiosity about the Jewish religion: it is reasonably likely to dissuade them, which will save them and others a considerable amount of time and trouble.

This book's description of itself as an impractical guide to conversion is accurate and sincere. A practical account of the process of conversion can be had from any Rabbinical authority approached for information (and this book gives some thoughts about whom to approach). This book is not meant as a structured handbook to take a person through the process; rather, it is a set of fairly random thoughts some or all of which may be helpful to those who are considering undergoing the conversion process, to those who have begun it and even perhaps to those who have completed it. The thoughts represent no more than the author's personal opinion, and are intended to be helpful and thought-provoking without being authoritative. To mis-quote the late Douglas Adams, the book is mostly apocryphal, or at least wildly inaccurate.

This book is also aimed in part at the Jewish community and establishment. It makes a number of fairly modest recommendations for change, based on the author's perception of a number of unnecessary and remediable imperfections of the way in which the conversion process is approached and operated at present.

The author has no very compelling qualification for writing this book. He knows a little about the operation of conversion in the United Kingdom, having been assigned as official tutor to about twenty conversion candidates of the London Beth Din over the past ten years, and having been involved informally in a number of other cases. He is not, however, in any sense an expert in the Jewish law of conversions (or of anything else) although he has one or two inklings. He has been involved in Jewish education of various kinds over the last twenty-five years or so, although only as an amateur. His professional interests lie in the field of secular law: he has served as a Government lawyer since 1988, first in the Lord Chancellor's Department and then as Parliamentary Counsel. He is now a part-time Parliamentary Counsel, and in the remainder of his professional time writes books, edits online legislation, acts as a freelance consultant on legislation and generally potters about getting in the way.

The author considers himself part of the orthodox Jewish community – that is to say, those who accept the authority of the tradition as expounded in the 16th century Shulchan Aruch code, which reflects Rabbinic developments since the Sinaitic revelation to Moses and has itself been subject to Rabbinic development, in each case by the Rabbis acting in accordance with their express scripturally-delegated authority. That community rejects the authenticity of "progressive" Judaism (including Reform, Liberal, Conservative and Masorti). This book is written from an orthodox point of view (at least according to the author, although in the nature of things others may disagree) and is not intended to present a balanced perspective.

There are only two other pieces of information that readers may require before beginning.

The first is that there is a very funny Jewish joke at the end of Question 9: if planning to give up before that Question, it is worth just taking in the joke before you put the book down.

The second is that the book is written, for the reader's convenience, as a series of more or less free-standing questions and answers, as a result of which certain issues are addressed in passing in more than one place.

Glossary of Hebrew Expressions

(Transliterated in a manner approximating to a mainstream Ashkenazi tradition.)

Ashkenazim – the Jews whose families come in recent history from, broadly, Germany, Poland, Russia and Lithuania. Principally contrasted with Sephardim (*q.v.*).

Beth Din – a Jewish religious court, normally consisting of three qualified Rabbis.

Botei Din – plural of Beth Din.

Bris Miloh – circumcision complying with Jewish law.

Chareidim – a (plural) word used, both by themselves and others, to designate the extreme right-wing of the Jewish religious political spectrum (including, but not limited to, the Chassidim). The principal contrast is between the chareidim and the dati leumi (*q.v.*).

Chassidim; Chassidus; Chassidish – the orthodox Jews most noted by others for their long black coats and brown fur hats, which reflect the clothing of the Polish nobility of the eighteenth century; the philosophy adhered to by Chassidim; appertaining to Chassidim.

Cohen – a Jewish man whose father was also a Cohen: sometimes translated as "priest" (not very helpfully). A Cohen has duties and privileges in relation to the Temple when extant. Even in the abeyance of the Temple service, Jewish law and thought require the Cohen to be treated with respect and impose some duties and restrictions on his behaviour.

Cohanim – plural of Cohen.

Dati leumi – the modern orthodox communities, principally contrasted with the Chareidim (*q.v.*). While they vary in their reasoning and ideas, the broad common denominator is an acceptance of the desirability of contributing to, and selectively benefiting from, the modern world.

Dayan – a Rabbinic judge; a member of a Beth Din.

Dayonim – plural of Dayan.

Ger; gerim; gerus – A convert; converts (plural noun); the process of converting.

Get – a document of Jewish divorce.

Giyoret – the female form of the word Ger (*q.v.*) although as an abstract "ger" is able to refer to both male and female converts.

Halachah – Jewish law.

Kashrus – the laws about kosher (*q.v.*) food.

Kesubah – a document of Jewish marriage.

Kippah – a small hat worn by Jewish males.

Kipod – Hebrew for hedgehog (for obvious reasons, not found in this book outside this glossary).

Kosher – permitted to be eaten in accordance with Jewish law; sometimes used in a more general sense to mean lawful or appropriate.

Mikveh – deep bath of a kind used in accordance with Jewish law for immersion by: converts as the culmination of the conversion process; married Jewish women monthly; most orthodox Jewish men at least once a year (in some communities much more frequently, even weekly).

Rabbi – a Jewish communal leader or teacher; strictly, the term is reserved for one who has been authorised by another Rabbi to render decisions in matters of Jewish law. But the term is often also assumed or applied as an informal mark of respect.

Sephardim – the Jews whose families come in recent history from, mostly, Iraq, Iran, Morocco, Turkey, Egypt, Spain, Portugal and Italy. Principally contrasted with Ashkenazim (*q.v.*).

Shabbos – the Sabbath day, on which orthodox Jews refrain from most kinds of constructive activity; it is spent largely in the synagogue and around the meal table.

Shiduch – an arranged marriage; also a meeting arranged as part of the process leading up to an arranged marriage.

Shul – a synagogue.

Torah – the Hebrew name for the five books of the Old Testament; it is also used to designate the Biblical and Rabbinic laws, taken together.

Yeshivah; yeshivot – a Talmudic academy; the plural form of the word. It is customary for boys to spend a year or two in yeshivah after finishing high school. Some stay on for longer because they cannot think of anything more useful to do and want to hide from the world. Others stay on for longer because they wish to pursue useful communal careers, whether as Rabbis, teachers or otherwise, for which Rabbinic ordination or other intensive study is required. Others stay on simply because their heart and soul is in the learning of Torah.

Yom Tov – the generic term for the festival days, which are observed in a manner similar to Shabbos (*q.v.*).

Question 1 – Why would anyone want to become Jewish?

There are three reasons for becoming Jewish; or to put it another way, prospective candidates fall into three classes:

(1) "regularisation cases",

(2) "marriage cases", and

(3) "real" converts.

The class of "regularisation cases" is the class of people who have for one reason or another grown up thinking of themselves as Jewish, and find out later that they are not, or at least not according to everybody. Question 2 explores this group further.

The class of "marriage cases" is the class of people who want to marry a Jewish man or woman, and find that the only way this can be achieved without causing a family or social catastrophe is to convert. Contrary to popular misconception, although it might be thought that someone wanting to convert in order to marry can be *ipso facto* thought not to have a genuine and independent commitment to Judaism, there is no objection on the part of most mainstream orthodox Botei Din to receive a convert under these conditions (subject to issues explored in Question 3). Indeed, for the London Beth Din this class (including its overlap with the "regularisation cases") forms a very sizeable proportion of the cases on the files at any time.

The class of "real" converts is the most baffling of all. However many converts and prospective converts one has met, it is always a surprise to meet someone with no previous link to the community who wants to become Jewish otherwise than for some obvious practical motive such as marriage. The non-Jewish communities of the world present many and varied opportunities for spiritual development, whether on humanitarian or religious bases; and many of today's Jewish communities present a very poor appearance to the outside world judged by any humanly accessible moral or ethical standards; taking these two facts together it is extremely baffling that anyone should want to join the community.

It is true that there are a small number of orthodox Jews whose religious observance makes them so thoroughly impressive and loveable that it would not be surprising if some non-Jews who saw them wanted to convert. The Talmud teaches that at any one time there are thirty-six perfectly righteous people in the world – and those of us who have met any one of them can readily understand how they might attract converts, in the same way as, according to tradition, Abraham and Sarah did at the beginning of the establishment of the Jewish religion. But these few spiritually perfect Jews are so retiring, and their occupations so limited, that they come into too little contact with non-Jews to be likely to be directly responsible for attracting many prospective converts.

The result is that it will never be easy to understand the class of "real converts"; and from their nature it is even more difficult to generalise about them than about the regularisation and marriage cases: each case can be understood only by reference to his or her personal background and circumstances. But some tentative thoughts about the class as a whole are offered in Question 4.

Question 2 – How do "regularisation" cases arise?

The first and most common reason why people might wish to become Jewish is that they thought they already were.

Many people are brought up within a Jewish community and are taught to think of themselves as wholly Jewish; then suddenly they discover that there is something about their ancestry that makes them technically non-Jewish by the standards applied by the orthodox Jewish community. This normally occurs when the person wants to marry within an orthodox synagogue: on being asked by the synagogue secretary to produce his or her parents' marriage certificate, it emerges that the parents were not married according to orthodox rites, generally because one or other of them was not Jewish according to orthodox standards.

Within this class of candidate for conversion will be the sons and daughters of women who converted under the auspices of a non-orthodox Jewish group and went on to marry Jewish men, in a non-orthodox synagogue: indeed, the conversion may have been undertaken purely in order to allow the marriage. After the wedding, it is very common for the couple to live within a United Synagogue or similarly traditional mid-stream orthodox community in which the husband was brought up. On the strength of the husband's known Jewish parentage the couple are accepted, to a greater or lesser extent, within the traditional community – and they attend synagogue along with everyone else. They may even have children who frequent Jewish schools or youth groups, mixing on terms of absolute and unquestioned equality of status with other Jewish children. Their deficient status remains overlooked, and probably imperfectly comprehended, in the corner of their parents' minds, until it obtrudes itself unpleasantly on what should be the happy occasion of their wishing to register themselves for a marriage in the orthodox synagogue. At that point the synagogue secretary requests the parents' certificate of orthodox marriage, and the whole story begins to unwind.

Also in this class are those whose mothers did not convert to Judaism through a non-orthodox community, but were born to those who did, or were born into families whose Jewish status was an acknowledged family fact, but not one recorded or tested within recent memory. It is surprising how quickly family records can become unattainable or questionable when the family in question came from nineteenth or early-twentieth century Eastern Europe. If two or three generations have lived their lives on the assumption that they are Jewish but without finding the need to present themselves for verification (perhaps being married in civil ceremonies and buried or cremated on municipal premises) their children will find it difficult or impossible to prove their Jewish status should they decide to contract a marriage in an orthodox synagogue.

It will be appreciated, although not perhaps comprehended, that in all these cases it is only those whose mothers' status is questionable who are in any difficulty. By orthodox Jewish law, the child of a Jewish mother is Jewish whether he or she likes it or not, while the child of a non-Jewish mother is non-Jewish, irrespective of the father's status. Upbringing is irrelevant, as are the aspirations of parents or child. On this point the law is entirely inflexible. Whether it has always been so is open to question: certainly, the orthodox understanding is that since the formal creation of the Jewish people as a nation by the transmission of the commandments to Moses on Mount Sinai over two thousand years ago, Jewish status has been determined upon birth by reference to the mother's status, subject only to the possibility of conversion. Before that time it is at least arguable that conversion was, to say the least, a less formal process than it has become today. Non-orthodox groups of Jews, including those who style themselves Reform and Liberal, take a more flexible attitude to Jewish status: but this flexibility is unequivocally rejected by all orthodox communities as being without basis in

Jewish law or practice (we are rather good at being unequivocal).

This situation results in a number of anomalies. For example, the child of two parents who were brought up in traditional Jewish households, married in an orthodox synagogue and have never been back since, will be able to marry in an orthodox synagogue. But a child whose mother was converted and married by the Reform movement, and whose parents have since their marriage been bastions of the father's orthodox community, perhaps attending synagogue three times every Saturday and sometimes during the week as well, will be unable to marry in that or any other orthodox synagogue, being technically not Jewish.

These anomalies, and it would be possible to describe any number of variations on the central theme that status and religious observance are far from coterminous, can appear startling and even brutal judged by humanitarian standards. They can be explained only by the assertion that the rules which cause them are not subject to humanitarian control – an assertion upon which I expand later on, but which is not likely to carry much weight with anyone outraged by the potential for human misery endemic in situations of the kind outlined above.

When a person finds himself or herself caught by one of these rules, and therefore in a position of not being technically Jewish according to orthodox standards but needing to be for marriage or for some other particular purpose, what follows depends on the nature of the individual concerned and on the precise family and other circumstances. Initially there is bound to be an element of shock, and shock affects different people in different ways. Similarly, a feeling of rejection by a community to which one thought that one belonged makes some people want to walk away, while it encourages others to try harder to assert membership. And it is not only the individual's own feelings that are likely to determine their reaction to their situation: the fiancé, for example, may have strong feelings along the lines of "Well if the orthodox don't want us, let's get married in the Reform the same way your parents were – what's the difference?" Or the individual's parents may suggest something similar, perhaps wanting to avoid or soften the suggestion that by their own behaviour they have created a difficulty for their child in marrying the partner of his or her dreams. For whatever reason, the reaction may well take the form of walking away from orthodoxy and towards any group, nominally Jewish, that appears prepared to accept and even welcome the proposed marriage. If so, that may be the end of the matter: and the couple and their descendants are quite likely to be lost to the orthodox Jewish community for ever. A great loss for them and for the community, however one chooses to apportion blame for it.

The alternative reaction is to decide to have the person's Jewish status "regularised". Although this sounds like a relatively small and easy matter, somehow less troublesome than a "real" conversion, the orthodox Beth Din approached to handle the conversion will quickly make it clear that for the purposes of Jewish law this has to be as much a real conversion as if the person had enjoyed no contact with the Jewish community in the whole of his or her previous life. The individual has to embark on a process that, as described later on, can reasonably be expected to take a number of years, at a time when he or she is anxious to hurry on with plans for a wedding that has suddenly become impracticable.

The stress on all concerned can only be imagined; it is surprising how many people manage to withstand it and come through the process with their actual and prospective family associations not strained beyond breaking-point. And yet people not only survive it but, if they can come to see it as an opportunity and not merely a crashing nuisance, emerge from the process having benefited from it considerably. The educational process that they are required to submit to has the ability to turn them, if they want to use it for this purpose, into knowledgeable and confident Jews, able to draw immense spiritual strength and value from their religion and at the same time able to make their religious observance an asset in their participation in the modern secular world. It may take some time for this aspect of affairs to present itself, but many who have completed the process are able to look back on it as a blessing in disguise, despite the initial potency of the disguise.

Question 3 – How do "marriage" cases arise?

The first class of prospective converts, the "regularisation" cases, stumble across the need to convert without any fair warning, so to speak. In the second class, at least one of the two parties involved either knows or generally could have been expected to know what they were getting into. This is the case where a boy or girl of unimpeachable Jewish status decides to marry a girl or boy who comes completely from outside the Jewish community.

There are many different ways in which this situation can come about. As a general rule, every Jewish boy or girl from an evenly remotely orthodox religious family knows from a very early age that he or she ought to choose their eventual marriage partner from within the Jewish community. If this makes the Jewish community sound exclusive and isolationist, that is the truth: there is nothing in classic Jewish thought that allows us to think of ourselves as being inherently better than anyone else (although one might be excused for gaining a contrary impression from the demeanour of a number of Jews) – but there is much in classic Jewish thought that requires us to think of ourselves as different from others, separated not by innate superiority of any kind but by the inheritance of a centuries-old religious tradition which is at once a challenge, a burden, a delight and an opportunity. To found a successful and committed Jewish marriage, with the aim of establishing a Jewish family, requires the union of two people who share this inheritance: hence the strong and eternal Jewish prejudice against intermarriage with other communities.

Despite this, Jewish boys and girls regularly and predictably fall in love with non-Jewish girls and boys. Commonly, this is a result or by-product, rather than a cause, of religious rebellion: the boy or girl has already strayed sufficiently far from the paths of religious observance to have entered into unconstrained social intercourse with the world at large. Perhaps a boy or girl has entered university, being released for the first time from the unattractive rigours of a home where orthodoxy is practised in a form that is less than appealing: looking around, the frank and honest behaviour of the previously feared outside world may present an intoxicatingly refreshing contrast to the closed and narrow-minded world from which he or she has come, perhaps exposing hitherto unsuspected strands of practical hypocrisy or intellectual double-dealing.

For whatever reason, once a Jewish boy or girl has set his or her heart on marrying a non-Jewish girl or boy, a range of options is open to them, in the same way as in the "regularisation" cases.

The most obvious course is to choose an entirely civil ceremony: but here, an unexpected and unaccountable obstacle often arises. The Jewish parents, who have not set foot inside a synagogue since their own marriage, and who have given their children no reason whatsoever to be proud of, interested in or even more than vaguely aware of their Jewish traditions, suddenly and without warning or apparent reason come over all religious, and raise objections to their son or daughter marrying a non-Jewish girl or boy. Homes without a single trace of religious observance suddenly resound with strangled sobs of "what would your grandmother have said?" And there is the rub – the parents have actively abandoned a tradition which they knew to have been precious to their grandparents or perhaps great-grandparents: but they encountered little resistance provided they submitted themselves to the religious jurisdiction for all their life-passage events: while they were married in synagogue themselves, and while they attended all important family burials and the occasional family bar mitzvah, their own parents saw them not as having strayed irrevocably from the Jewish tradition, but merely as representing the natural inclination of the younger generation to go out and make the best of the outside world. Probably their own parents and grandparents were proud of the ease with which their children and grandchildren succeeded in blending into, and obtaining wealth and status in, what was once an unattainable world of comfort and prosperity; and so they saw their drifting away from Jewish practice without alarm.

But now the next generation has come along, with virtually no memory at all of real religious practices in the house, and possibly no actual memories of the grandparents or great-grandparents to whom the distinction between Jews and non-Jews was a practical daily reality based on religious conviction. And it looks with bewilderment at parents who, having encouraged it in no way to practice or even remember anything of significance in the way of religious life, suddenly react with unaccountable alarm at the prospect of intermarriage in the family. The child involved may even have been living with a non-Jewish boyfriend or girlfriend for some years without encountering any significant opposition from the parents: but suddenly the air resounds with "marriage is different …"

What happens next depends, again, on the individual strengths, weaknesses and inclinations of each of the people involved. As in the "regularisation" case, the most extreme reaction at one end of the scale is for the children to ignore their parents' objections and go ahead with the civil ceremony, or even with a church or other religious ceremony where their chosen partner's family has more practical connection with their religion than the Jewish side do with theirs. That may or may not cause an unbridgeable rift with the Jewish parents: probably not these days – a few bouts of hysterics, a few slammed telephone receivers, followed by gradual but effective reconciliation. As with the "regularisation" case, however, the real rift is between the Jewish child and his or her religious tradition of a few thousand years. While there are some nominally Jewish groups which will extend a welcome to the couple in the unlikely event of their wishing any sort of contact with the Jewish community, all realistic prospect of any useful connection with the authentic orthodox traditions of their religion is lost: the frail cords of tradition, stretched gossamer thin by the wilful carelessness of one or more generations of parents, are finally snapped by the entirely reasonable and understandable behaviour of the child. Any further generations, although nominally Jewish if descending from an unbroken female line, will in all likelihood not even be sufficiently aware of their Jewish antecedents ever to think of trying to find a way back. Of course, miracles do happen – but we do not rely on them.

Next to that extreme reaction are various others. One obvious compromise is to marry through one of the nominally Jewish groups who abandon tradition in allowing themselves complete flexibility in whom they choose to regard as Jewish and what they regard as acceptable matrimonial alliances. They may offer the non-Jewish partner a conversion, of a kind which as we have seen will be regarded as completely ineffective in any of the orthodox Jewish communities world-wide: but they will not insist even on that. If the couple choose to marry in a civil ceremony at a registry office the Reform or other group will still welcome them and their children to synagogue, to school and in any other way afterwards. But the door to the orthodox community is shut for the couple and their children, to be opened only by the painful and disruptive process of "regularisation" described above.

Although there are many other possible stops along the road of compromise, the only real alternative to the extreme of simply walking away from the Jewish tradition is to embark on the process of having the non-Jewish fiancé or fiancée convert through the orthodox establishment. As in the case of regularisation, easier said than done. For one thing, again, this is not something that can be accomplished in a few months at the same time as hiring the hall and matching the colours of table linen for the reception: if the couple choose this path they are also effectively choosing to put on hold their wedding plans for what at the outset must necessarily be an indeterminate number of years. Much to ask of any young couple, but particularly so in the common case of youngsters who may have been living together or seeing each other for a few years, and who have now decided to settle down and start a family. However softly the biological clock is ticking, its voice is loud enough to be heard and to cause dismay at the prospect of "anything up to a few years" delay. What was a casual assurance that they could start wall-papering the nursery now and hope to have it occupied in a year's time suddenly has to be confronted and abandoned in favour of a distinctly uncertain future.

Despite this, a considerable number of young men and women have the courage to go through this process. For some it may be, or may start out as, merely a need to pacify an unpredictably hysterical prospective mother-in-law or angry prospective father-in-law: but that is rarely enough in itself to cause the couple to start out on, or to stay the course of, the long and demanding process of conversion: in all the cases that I have encountered, at least at some point the process becomes one in which the couple are inspired by a genuine desire, on one side, not to abandon centuries of Jewish heritage, and, on the other, to embrace a new spiritual tradition.

Of course, some couples go through a civil marriage and then look for a form of "regularisation" by having the non-Jewish partner go through conversion soon after it. They may argue to themselves that this way they keep everyone happy: the caterer can go ahead with the plans for an immediate wedding, but the parents' vague warnings about losing the next generation to Judaism are effectively countered. By the time any children come along, both parents will be safely Jewish with a status sufficient to satisfy the most exacting of orthodox tests. As will be seen later on, however, the process is rarely quite so accommodating. Two things are sufficient to say about this course now. First, unless the process is completed before the first child is born, then (in the case where the non-Jewish partner is the mother) the child will nominally convert along with the mother: the result is that the child's status is that of a convert which in the case of a daughter brings a significant restriction of her later choice of husband, as will be discussed further below. Secondly, although some couples are encouraged to undergo the civil marriage first on the grounds that they are told it will, in effect, force the religious authorities to accelerate the conversion process, they afterwards find out that this is far from the case, and that they have made their situation more complicated rather than less.

As a footnote to the marriage cases, it is worth observing that there is a small class who seek to convert after marriage for a particular ulterior motive, not related to the marriage itself or any actual or possible children. Halachah prohibits the burial of a non-Jew in a specifically Jewish graveyard. There are therefore occasional cases of couples (married at civil law only, or possibly at civil law followed by a non-orthodox religious ceremony) consisting of one halachically-Jewish spouse and one non-Jewish spouse, who have lived happily together for years or even decades without suffering any inconvenience from the irregularity of status. In one case the couple were well-respected members of an orthodox synagogue for many years, the other members of which had no idea that either partner was not Jewish. They continued in this fashion quite contentedly until they were nearing old age, at which point they approached the Beth Din with a view to regularising one spouse's status purely so that they could eventually be buried together. Possibly surprisingly, the Beth Din not only countenanced the conversion but were quite moderate in their demands in the matter of life-style changes.

Question 4 – Why does anyone want to become a "real" convert?

Whatever the individual circumstances, the classes of "marriage" cases and of "regularisation" cases generally deserve a considerable amount of sympathy and understanding. They can reasonably be seen as the unwitting victims of the behaviour of previous generations (although their degree of wittingness varies). The next class, however, deserves no sympathy at all, for reasons that will shortly become clear.

The final class of prospective converts is that of the "real" converts: those who have neither a family connection nor a social connection with Judaism to begin with, nor a prospective marriage or other practical motive for wishing to convert. So what makes them do it?

The obvious answer that leaps to mind on first pondering the question is that they must all be stark raving bonkers. Having met many of them over the years the author has come to the conclusion that first thoughts are, as always, quite sound: all "real" converts are mad, but their madness is almost always of an extraordinarily precious, creative and inspiring kind. The madness that the Jewish people showed in trundling happily into the desert leaving the wealth and profusion of ancient Egypt for the prospect of joining their leader Moses in an early death by spear or starvation, is the same madness that the "real" convert shows in joining the Jewish community in each generation. A naivety, a lack of practical sense, and an absurd trust that the beauty and ideals of Judaism are worth living and dying for despite the spiritual poverty of many of their apparent exponents: not all of us can aspire to be as mad as that.

The Talmud (Kidushin 70b) famously says of converts that they are "as damaging to the people of Israel as a scab" basing itself on a play of words in two Biblical contexts. As a passing comment not obviously explained by the material before or after it, this comment has given rise to a number of different Rabbinic explanations over the years. Broadly speaking, they are classifiable into two groups: the first, derogatory in some way about converts, doubting their sincerity or durability; the second, derogatory in some way about the Jewish people. The essence of the second group of explanations is that by comparison with converts, those born into Judaism as a generality come out a very poor second.

The latter explanation of the Talmud's comments certainly conforms to the author's feelings based on the "real" converts he has known. Their devotion to the service of God, the sacrifices they make happily and in order to achieve their goal of accepting the enormous burden of the Torah's commandments, and their spiritual energy, all inspire an uncomprehending admiration. While contrasting their pure attitude to their adoptive religion with the nonchalance, complacency and hypocrisy which are so endemic to a considerable proportion of all sections of the indigenous orthodox community, one can easily see the Talmud encouraging us to make the comparison for ourselves and to feel a constructive sense of shame, as well as a determination to do better, as a result of the unattractive contrast.

In a sense, this comparison deepens my lack of understanding of why these few individuals choose to join us. If one were looking throughout the world for an obviously and conspicuously spiritual society, orthodox Jewry would not be an obvious choice. There is nothing about the apparent behaviour of any large sector of the orthodox Jewish world as a whole that would appear likely to inspire the admiration or even approval of the casual observer from outside. The thirty-six wholly righteous of each generation remain firmly self-hidden from all but the most penetrating inquirer, while as a rule the more spiritually inspiring members of the orthodox community are also those with, designedly, the lowest public profile. Of course there are a number of exceptional members of the orthodox community whose public prominence is combined with an obvious commitment to a sincere and balanced observance of the Torah as a whole – and one can readily understand that encounters with them might make someone interested in finding out about Judaism: but there are also many, often those with the highest profile, who would only put people off.

One could easily understand someone being attracted by the face of a modern orthodox community in Israel, in particular, where for a large number of people Judaism flourishes as a powerful way of life combining spiritual energy and enthusiastic involvement in the modern world: but few non-Jews are exposed to communities of that kind. In the United Kingdom the most public of the different faces of the orthodox communities are not such as to attract much in the way of admiration, let alone emulation. Too many orthodox Jews, both from modern and from chareidi communities, have a prominent profile by reason of their criminal, exploitative or otherwise objectionable business practices; conspicuous wealth and extravagant consumption are more obvious trademarks of the publicly observable face of the orthodox than spiritual commitment and moral achievement. While there are many inspiring individuals, and even small communities and movements, whose opposition to the march of materialism is their principal guiding motive, they are few and generally retiring, and their face is rarely seen or recognised, even by those within the community and still less by those outside.

So in the end what is it that impels most of those "real" converts who find their way to the religious authorities in Europe or America as candidates for conversion? God knows. Of course, there will be some who wish to belong to what they see as a close-knit, supportive community, and whose desire to belong is the conscious or sub-conscious but decisive motive in their conversion. But social factors are not, of course, a sufficient reason for accepting a person as a convert; nor in itself would they be sufficient for most people to subject themselves to the troublesome process, and equally burdensome result, of conversion. So in the end one is simply left to absorb the awe-inspiring fact that a small number of people in every generation see the spark of divinity emanating from the practice of Judaism as they observe it, or as they have learned about it, and come to join the people whom God chose some thousands of years ago as His nation. Once there, they frequently set standards of devotion that cause the rest of us to stand humbled and ashamed, and that elevate them to positions of leadership and inspiration. It was not only King David who was descended from recently-converted stock, although he is traditionally advanced as the foremost example; in every generation converts have been leading scholars, Rabbis and communal workers of all kinds.

A Rabbinic story has it that before God offered the Torah to the Jewish people at Mount Sinai, He offered it to all other nations in turn, and each one refused it on the grounds of a particular aspect that they found uncongenial. A gloss on this story adds that within each nation there were a small number of individuals who would have been prepared and even anxious to accept the challenge – but it was being offered only to a people who would all accept it "with one heart, like one person". The tradition adds that the souls of these individuals are reincarnated and become, in later generations, those who join the Jewish people through conversion. I love this tradition, and it seems a fitting place to end my discussion of the inspiring enigma that is the convert: they come to Judaism because it is never truly foreign to them; it lights the spark of perception of the holiness of God's Torah that was kindled in their soul at the time of Mount Sinai, and that has smouldered ever since. In that sense, they were never truly outsiders and they have not really converted from one thing to another: they are my lost brothers and sisters who have at last come home. *Sholom aleichem* – welcome back!

Question 5 – What exactly is conversion?

Today, conversion is a formal and rigid process, controlled by the Botei Din. Immersion in a mikveh marks the moment of transition from non-Jew to Jew, at which point the convert formally accepts upon himself or herself to observe all the laws of the Torah; and a formal certificate of the Beth Din is then issued to attest to the transition. Prior to that, in the United Kingdom at least, a course of study, involving at least one tutor and a number of oral examinations along the way, follows a set syllabus in preparing the prospective convert to lead an active Jewish life. Any Beth Din that offers conversion as one of its services, runs a more or less formal process of tuition for conversion; a number of Botei Din do not offer conversion, generally for reasons of size or desire for communal unity, and these will redirect inquiries to one that does.

It seems likely, however, that the degree of formality attending conversion has increased considerably over the years. In particular, when Judaism was purely a religion, rather than a nation, its creator Abraham and his wife Sarah are said to have "converted" a large number of people from the area of Haran (according to traditional Rabbinic commentaries on Genesis 12:5). This may have been a wholly informal process, without ceremony of any kind, but merely indicating those who had been influenced by Abraham and Sarah and as a result had adopted their uniquely monotheistic faith, together with all or some of their religious practices.

At what points and for what reasons the formalities grew is a matter for historians to conjecture and demonstrate. The fact that they were not always entirely as they are now, however, is important, because it shows that they are not the essence of what conversion is.

The Jewish faith is not owned by the Rabbis or anyone else, although the Rabbis play a Biblically ordained part in its development and regulation. Neither Abraham, who founded our religion, nor Moses, the prophet under whose leadership we formally accepted the Torah and became a nation, was entrusted by God with some kind of right to control who may or may not approach God. This has two important implications. First, anyone who genuinely and sincerely is determined to adopt the entirety of Torah Judaism cannot be prevented from becoming Jewish by any social, political, financial or other considerations on the part of the Jewish community, its Rabbis or any of its other members. Secondly, anyone who obtains a certificate of conversion from an orthodox Beth Din by going through the motions of the conversion process without a sincere intention to live a life as a Jew in accordance with the laws of the Torah as they affect every aspect of a person's dealings with God and other people, has merely obtained a worthless piece of paper.

The essence of conversion is therefore more about becoming part of the Jewish community than about being accepted within it. When the Dayonim sign a conversion certificate, they are not conferring a status which rests within their gift to grant; rather, they are providing written evidence on behalf of the community as a whole of three things: (i) that their observations of the behaviour of the person concerned leads them to believe that he or she is sincere in the wish to lead a Torah lifestyle; (ii) that the person has had an opportunity to acquire sufficient basic knowledge of Jewish law to begin to lead that lifestyle, subject to the continual need, which they share with the rest of us, to improve their knowledge and observance; and (iii) that the person has formally accepted the burden of the Torah and its commandments (which by express Biblical verse include acceptance of the authority of the Rabbis) and has marked that acceptance by undergoing ritual immersion in the mikveh.

That said, the process also confers a formal status that has some specific consequences in Jewish law. Most importantly, children born to a woman who has acquired the valid formal status of giyoret (female ger) are automatically possessed of full Jewish status at birth, irrespective of the state of the mother's religious observance when the child is born.

To give another example of the significance of acquisition of the status of ger, Jewish law prohibits the interment in a specifically Jewish burial ground of a person who is not Jewish. A non-Jew who lives in a Jewish family, perhaps with a Jewish civil spouse, and observes some or even all of the Jewish practices of that family, would not by that token be permitted to be interred in a Jewish cemetery. But a person who has completed the conversion process and concerning whose sincerity at the time of conversion there is no room for doubt, will be unreservedly accepted for interment in a Jewish cemetery even if their Jewish observance had somewhat slipped since the time of conversion.

It follows from the example of burial given above that another important aspect of the nature of the conversion process is that it is irreversible. Just as the Dayonim do not "give" conversion, they cannot take it away. A person who has converted in accordance with the process described below and who at the time made a genuine and sincere commitment to orthodox Judaism, does not cease to be Jewish by reason of their observance lapsing later; any more than a person born to a Jewish mother becomes non-Jewish by virtue of ceasing to practice Judaism. In both cases, they are seen in Jewish thought as full members of the Jewish community who are in effect waiting to be brought back to full Jewish observance when we can show them, by example, how rich and fulfilling a Torah lifestyle could be.

So what of the small number of highly publicised cases in which the Dayonim of one or another Beth Din have declared a conversion, normally carried out in a different country to that in which the Beth Din concerned is operating, invalid by reason of the convert's non-observance?

The answer is simply that in these cases something has happened to make the Dayonim doubt whether the conversion was ever a genuine one – whether there was ever an actual acceptance of the burden of the Torah, or whether the certificate issued at the time was, in effect, a piece of false evidence extracted from the Dayonim through a palpable fraud. More will be said later about the nature of Israeli "geographically limited" conversions; for now in describing the essence of a conversion all that needs to be said is that if a conversion is genuine at the time, it is irreversible – but that if later evidence shows clearly that the conversion was never genuine, it may at that later time be declared always to have been void.

That does not mean, of course, that gerim are or should be under constant supervision after the event to confirm their original sincerity: rather, it means that if something happens to cause the original conversion to be examined (such as turning up in a new country and asking for it to be recognised) the Dayonim will look into the circumstances of the conversion to ensure that there are no reasons to doubt whether it was ever genuine. But even if there is reason to examine the circumstances of the original conversion, unless there is serious reason to doubt the original sincerity of a conversion, a ger is entitled to the same presumption of legitimacy and sincerity that applies to all Jewish people in matters of status: "all Jews are under a presumption of kashrus" is a maxim of the Rabbis that is applied broadly to matters of status and beyond, and applies to all who form or appear to form part of the community. Someone who lives as part of the community and is accepted as such is entitled to the benefit of the presumption, and his or her status can be affected only by the very clearest evidence, not by rumour, however apparently compelling (see the responsum of Rabbi Moshe Feinstein, *Igros Moshe*, Yoreh Deoh 2:131).

Question 6 – How does the process work today in the United Kingdom?

Let us take the mythical case of a person who lives in any place in the United Kingdom outside London, whether it be a small rural village in Hertfordshire or the middle of a residential estate in a suburb of Coventry. He or she for some reason or other becomes interested in Judaism and forms the idea that they might possibly want to convert. What should they do?

In dealing with the early stages – up to making contact with a Beth Din – I am addressing only the case of the "real" convert – not the "regularisation" or "marriage" case. Someone who has already had considerable exposure to the Jewish community and wants to convert in order to regularise his or her status or to enable him or her to marry their Jewish girlfriend or boyfriend should simply approach the local orthodox Rabbi as quickly as possible and be as open and honest as possible. To pretend that their only reason for aspiring to convert is that they have begun to develop an interest in orthodox Judaism for some reason or other, is only going to waste everybody's time and may prejudice their chances of success in the long term. Sooner or later in the process it is bound to emerge that they have some Jewish involvement; and the existence of a Jewish girlfriend or boyfriend is something that they will not be able to keep quiet during the entire process from start to finish. If, however, a convert was successful in hiding the existence of a Jewish boyfriend or girlfriend from the Beth Din during the whole of the conversion process, and triumphantly turned around after the conversion and made plans for a wedding, it is likely that the Dayonim would consider the entire conversion to have been undergone under false pretences, nullifying it and making the conversion certificate worthless. So the only sensible thing to do is to approach the Beth Din and tell the whole story as early as possible. The prospective convert who is open with the Beth Din should find that the Beth Din is open with them; they might not like everything they are told, but at least everyone will know what they are dealing with at the beginning, and nasty surprises should be capable of being avoided altogether.

Reverting to the case of the "real" convert, the starting point is to find out as much as possible from the resources available to you. Until a few years ago, this was good advice which was easier to give than to take much advantage of; a local library might have or be able to obtain a few rudimentary books about Jewish practice, but probably nothing very detailed or very reliable. And it is impossible anyway to gain a feel for the realities of Jewish observance from books. Nowadays, however, as well as the greater availability of a variety of authoritative books on the subject, most people have some kind of access to the internet; and if they use that intelligently it can be a real window on many different aspects of Jewish religious life, both in this country and abroad.

If the initial research that a person does confirms his or her initial feeling of interest, it is now time to make human contact. If you know of a local orthodox synagogue, there is no reason why you should not simply turn up there unannounced at around nine o'clock on a Saturday morning and see what is going on; the Sabbath morning service is likely to start at around that time and is likely to last for something in the region of two or two and a half hours. If in doubt, it is not an orthodox synagogue if men and women are sitting together for the service; if they are not, it is probably an orthodox service (although not certainly – there are some non-orthodox groups who separate for services, but you would find that out in due course when you became a little more involved). Turning up unannounced is probably not a bad idea, in fact, so long as you don't expect to get too much out of the experience, and so long as you are not embarrassed to tell anyone who comes up to be friendly that you are not Jewish and are just looking around, if they don't mind. They shouldn't mind, but don't expect them to be too friendly either; apart from the fact that there are security concerns nowadays (and so don't be surprised if they want to know your name and address or if they ask to have their security officer check your bag, for example) since Judaism is a non-proselytising religion nobody will feel that they ought to be welcoming your interest and encouraging it. Indeed, you are likely to be made to feel distinctly out of place, which ought not to worry you too much so long as you expect it from the outset.

If you do not feel you would be comfortable just turning up at a synagogue out of the blue, you need to make contact with someone involved in the local orthodox community, preferably the Rabbi. Even if you do decide to visit the synagogue once or twice on the off-chance, after that you will also need to make contact with someone in the community, and it is probably better not to try to do that in the course of an unannounced visit.

Finding your local orthodox Rabbi or synagogue may not be entirely easy, even in these days of the internet – for one thing, if you live anywhere outside one of the few largest towns in the United Kingdom, the chances are that you do not have a local orthodox synagogue! Fifty years or so ago there were orthodox communities of some considerable size in most largish towns and cities of the United Kingdom; and a number still have communities, although many are ageing as the youngsters move away either from Judaism or from the area or from both. The only places with large Jewish communities now are London and Manchester, with sizeable communities still in Newcastle, Birmingham, Leeds, Cardiff, Bournemouth and one or two other places. If you live in any of these places you will either already have noticed where the synagogue is or will not find it hard to find.

Outside these areas your search is going to be harder. Your starting point should be to contact the United Synagogue – via its website – and inquire whether there is a synagogue which is part of or affiliated to the United Synagogue anywhere near you. The United Synagogue is the largest orthodox synagogue body in the United Kingdom, not counting the Chareidi communities in Stamford Hill, some parts of North West London, Manchester and Gateshead. The United Synagogue may be able to point you towards a smallish but vibrant local Jewish community, and give you the details of a local Rabbi to contact.

If you find that you have a local orthodox community, your next step is to contact the Rabbi, preferably by making an appointment to go and talk to him at some convenient time during the week. When you meet him, you will take the opportunity to tell him about your interest in Judaism. He will want to know how long your interest has lasted, and what practical steps you have taken so far to finding out about Jewish practice. Probably, he will have to set you right on a number of points where you have, entirely reasonably, picked up a variety of misinformation from sites on the internet or from Jewish friends and acquaintances, many of whom know less than nothing about their own religion.

At that meeting you should ask the Rabbi whether he minds if you start to attend the synagogue on Saturday mornings. He is unlikely to be desperately enthusiastic about the idea. Probably he will see this as his first opportunity to show the kind of practical discouragement which is generally seen as the most effective way of filtering out all but those whose desire to become Jewish is the most sincere. This principle, which will begin to be applied by the local Rabbi and will last almost until the end of your contact with the Beth Din, has always seemed to me to be suspect, and I discuss it further in Question 16.

One way or another, however, and with a greater or lesser degree of enthusiasm and welcome, you will find your way from time to time to the local synagogue on a Saturday morning. By this point you will have found and read enough by way of a "basic guide" to Judaism to have a thoroughly misleading idea of what to expect. The more you have read or been told about the Saturday morning service, the more surprised you will be by the reality. Much will depend, of course, on where you are: if your local synagogue is a small community somewhere outside London and Manchester, you are likely to find it fairly orderly and decorous, with a sense of respect and purpose, and probably fairly friendly and welcoming as well. If you are close to any of the main centres of orthodoxy in London or Manchester and you venture into any of the small orthodox synagogues there, your main problem will be to distinguish the service from the social hubbub taking place around you.

In a busy orthodox synagogue you may find that there is no need to explain yourself and your position because nobody takes any notice of you. Hopefully, however, even in a large and busy synagogue sooner or later someone will approach you, even if only to offer you somewhere to sit. If you are attending as a result of having agreed with the local Rabbi that you may, it would be as well to try to arrange to meet him at the start of the service (at which time you and he will probably be almost the only people there); if he can brief one or two central people about you, you will be spared the embarrassment of having to explain yourself, or of any of the misunderstandings that can arise (such as being called up to the Torah reading without having the faintest idea that it is happening to you!). If the Rabbi with whom you have made contact is not there, you would be well advised to make your way to someone who looks sensible as soon as you arrive, explain that you are not Jewish and that you just wanted to attend the service to look around: even if the only result of that is that you are left alone, that will be a result worth achieving. Hopefully, however, it will bring a welcome and the offer of a seat, plus maybe even a little bit of guidance about what is happening during the service. If it brings none of those things, perhaps you can try a different synagogue the next time.

After a few visits to a local synagogue you will find that you are strongly encouraged to make some kind of formal arrangement. To put it bluntly, the orthodox community does not encourage regular involvement in services or other communal events of people who are neither Jewish nor accepted into a recognised conversion programme. The reasons are obvious, and well-justified. The most obvious is to do with relationships: the function of the synagogue has always been partly social and communal, as well as being a place for prayer: particularly in the case of single people, nothing is served by introducing them into a community when they are not in a position to mix freely and contract friendships which might turn into something more. So however welcoming the community and the Rabbi are, sooner rather than later you will be invited, hopefully in a polite and sensitive manner, either to cease your visits or to make formal contact with the London Beth Din for the purposes of becoming accepted as a candidate for conversion.

The next stage will be to obtain an official appointment with the London Beth Din, probably with the conversion registrar rather than with one of the Dayonim. Even to get to that point may be something of a bureaucratic struggle; but eventually you will surmount the hurdles and find yourself in the Beth Din.

The less you expect from the opening stages of the process the more likely your expectations are to be realised! In your first interview or other correspondence with the Beth Din you are likely to find that while you are anxious to get started and make speedy progress their principal concerns appear to be more to do with slowing you down and obstructing you.

For example, you may have discovered a number of interesting classes and courses offered by one or other of the Jewish learning centres in London and you may mention to the Beth Din how eager you are to sign up for them, expecting to be congratulated on making such spirited early progress: in fact, the reaction will be, at best, a concerned discussion about whether it is yet appropriate for you to be attending courses of that kind. There are two kinds of objection to be considered. First, there are the social issues discussed above in relation to attending synagogue regularly. Secondly, there are theological objections to teaching Torah to non-Jews: these do not prevent general explanations of the kind that is serviceable in inter-faith discussions, nor do they prevent intense practical instruction for someone accepted on a conversion programme: but even for conversion candidates at a fairly advanced stage, these objections require his or her studies to be kept to practical preparations for observance of Jewish law, including practical instruction in the basic tenets of faith, but excluding academic Talmudic or philosophical exercises. There may also be concerns about the reliability of the institution that you propose to attend: broadly speaking, the more exciting and interesting it appears the less likely it is to be regarded as entirely sound by the Beth Din! In general, the result is that you are likely to be encouraged at least for a considerable time to confine your studies to the tutor assigned by the Beth Din and to any books that he or she recommends.

Your tutor will in effect control your rate of progress to a considerable degree. But that is only once you have a tutor: a casual inquiry about conversion does not result in the assignment of a tutor, and broadly speaking you will be expected to have shown reliable signs of sincerity and determination to succeed before a tutor is assigned to you. If your arrival at the Beth Din is preceded by a considerable period of involvement in a local community with the encouragement and help of the local Rabbi, the period before assignment of a tutor might be very short, perhaps only a few weeks. But in other cases it is likely to be half a year or even longer before a tutor is assigned.

The assignment of a tutor is probably the most significant point in the entire conversion process before its completion. For one thing, it amounts to tacit acceptance by the Beth Din that you are reasonably serious about converting, at last so far as can be judged at that stage: if you are thought to be wholly insincere or not seriously committed, the Beth Din is unlikely to assign a tutor. For another thing, once you have a tutor you will be able to explain to people whom you meet in synagogue or elsewhere in a communal context that you are formally accepted on the London Beth Din's conversion programme and are studying under so-and-so as your official tutor. In addition, until you have a tutor there is a limit to how much real progress you can make in your studies: once you have a tutor, you can aim to accelerate the progress to a considerable degree, subject to certain constraints.

The first constraint is a practical one. As I have already said, it is impossible to learn practical Jewish observance from books, and there is a limit on how much one can learn it even in face to face study sessions with a knowledgeable and experienced tutor. The only effective way to learn what orthodox Jews do is to live with them, eat with them, pray with them, cook with them, shop with them and generally to participate in their everyday lives and conversations. But having said that, you will learn from your tutor more than you could ever learn from books and if your tutor is good, you should be able to move more or less as fast as you want at a theoretical level, provided that you are prepared to devote the necessary time and energy to your studies.

The "if your tutor is good" is the second constraint. There is no formal qualification to become a tutor for the London Beth Din. Some of the tutors, but not all by any means, are Rabbis – which means that they can be reasonably guaranteed to be knowledgeable, but it does not necessarily mean that they are skilled at imparting their knowledge to others. Since men are assigned to male tutors and women to female tutors, no female candidate is tutored by a Rabbi, and a Rabbi's wife is one step less guaranteed than her husband to be either knowledgeable or skilled as a teacher (although many are both, in some cases more so than their husbands). Of the tutors who are not Rabbis, many are professional and qualified teachers; again as a generalisation, these are likely to be effective and personable communicators. Others are merely well-meaning amateurs (at least in the sense that they are not formally qualified, but not necessarily in the sense that they do not charge for their services – as to which see further Question 10): it is necessarily the case that this last group is the most hit-and-miss class – an interest in interfering in other people's lives and telling them what to do is not in itself a guarantee of either a sufficiency of knowledge or an aptitude for imparting it; but of course an enthusiastic and conscientious amateur can be as effective as, or more effective than, many a professional.

Generalisations apart, it is as true in conversion tutoring as in other fields of teaching that a teacher who works well with one pupil may work less well with another. All of which brings me to my main point about tutors: it is essential that the conversion candidate remembers at all times that he or she is the "customer", at least in one sense of the word and probably in the commercial sense as well. If you are not satisfied that your tutor is providing what you need, it may be because he or she understands the process better than you do, but it may alternatively be because he or she is not a very good teacher, or at any rate not the right teacher for you. I have sometimes been contacted by conversion candidates dissatisfied with the rate of progress that their tutor is encouraging and enabling them to make: on discussing the nature of the sessions it has sometimes been clear that the tutor is entirely competent and is pursuing the studies at the only rate consistent with the candidate's knowledge and skills; but sometimes it has been at least likely that the tutor is not pursuing the course with the vigour and pace that the candidate is able to cope with and is therefore entitled to expect. Sometimes asking for an acceleration or for some other change in the course of studies produces the necessary result; but not always. Where the candidate feels that negotiation with the tutor is producing no change or insufficient change, he or she should feel entitled, and even encouraged, to approach the Beth Din to discuss the situation. A change of tutor should be easy to arrange, and there is no reason why a candidate should feel embarrassed at taking three or four attempts before settling with a tutor with whom they are happy; nor should there be any assumption that changing tutors even several times is in itself an indication of lack of commitment or gravity. Finally, it is important that neither the candidate nor anyone else should prioritise the feelings or finances of the tutor above the needs of the candidate: my most influential teacher who was in his time the most effective organiser of youth and adult education groups in the United Kingdom used to stress – one might have thought unnecessarily but in practice very necessarily – that educational programmes exist purely for the sake of the students, not to satisfy the teachers' egos: if a teacher is not up to the job, by insisting on continuing in post he or she is not only in effect stealing the money paid for a function that they are not fulfilling, but in the case of conversions is also risking the spiritual progress and well-being of another human being for selfish reasons.

Your assigned tutor will follow a syllabus set by the London Beth Din. The syllabus is a short document, about five pages in length, and you will be given a copy when your tutor is assigned if you have not already been given one earlier in the conversion process. The most striking thing about it for someone who knows little about Judaism is likely to be the apparent imbalance between the minutiae of ritual observance, which cover about ninety-five percent of the syllabus, and the fundamental tenets of Jewish belief. Nor is this misleading; the imbalance is likely to be greater rather than lesser when it comes to the division of actual teaching time and energy. This reflects the nature of orthodox Judaism, which is primarily a matter of observance: a typical scholar's bookshelves abound with texts and responsa on all matters of ritual observance and may contain just a few volumes of what a non-Jewish academic or scholar would recognise as philosophy or theology. One of the most oft-quoted phrases of the Torah is the Jewish people's reaction (Exodus 24:7) to the word of God "we will do and we will listen" – this is expounded by the Rabbis as amounting to " we will do and then we will come to understand" and it is rightly regarded generally as summarising the Jewish philosophy: you do not learn about the Sabbath and its meaning from books, but by sitting around a Sabbath table drinking in the atmosphere – and the same for all other aspects of Jewish ritual and observance. One result of this is that most Jews, including most scrupulously observant Jews who are well-versed in technical ritual minutia, are astonishingly ignorant of the basic theological principles of Judaism: if you absorb carefully the basic Rabbinic materials on the fundamental tenets described in the Beth Din syllabus you will rank as a theological expert within the Jewish community who could teach most "rank and file" Jews much about the nature of the religion that they and their families have practiced for generations – except that in all probability they would neither know nor care what you were talking about.

Your tutor will be with you until the end of your conversion process, unless you change him or her. Indeed, if the relationship works as well as it can do, you may find that you stay in touch with your tutor for the rest of your life. The relationship is a curious one. In one sense, the tutor is entirely "on your side" or, to put it more neutrally, he or she is there purely to facilitate your conversion process. Tutors do not make substantive decisions about the sincerity of prospective converts, their rate of progress or any other matter relevant to whether they will or will not be successful. But they do make reports to the Beth Din regularly about what material has been covered, and they are asked for a general opinion about the candidate's commitment to his or her studies and the rate at which the material appears to be being absorbed. Sometimes the tutor will be consulted more generally, but the distinction is always rigidly preserved whereby the Dayonim are solely responsible for making decisions.

The result is that you ought to be able to feel fairly relaxed with your tutor, and you ought not be made to feel that he or she is judging you. You ought to be able to ask him or her anything and to tell them anything. At my first meeting with a new candidate it has been my practice to emphasise that our sessions are confidential in the same way as are appointments with a doctor or any other professional; not just the content of the sessions but even the fact of them is confidential – I would no more tell a friend or acquaintance of someone I was tutoring that I was doing so than my doctor would tell my friend that I had come to see him professionally. At one stage I had two members of the same synagogue – both Jewish men who wanted to marry non-Jewish women who were therefore assigned tutors to learn alongside their fiancées – coming to see me, and although they knew each other well in synagogue neither ever heard me so much as mention the other. So in that sense the sessions are in complete confidence. But the sessions are not confidential in another sense, in that the candidate always knows that the tutor is required periodically to report back to the Beth Din. I always remind my candidates not to tell me anything that they would not want mentioned to the Beth Din; and in one or two cases there has been as a result a self-imposed restraint on the candour of communication between us, resulting in the end in a less helpful service from me to the candidate.

If you are able to be entirely open with your tutor, you will hopefully find him or her an invaluable resource. You are likely to meet his or her family, and to a greater or lesser extent you may even become part of it. Time spend around your tutor's Sabbath or festival table with their family, observing and participating, may be some of the most valuable educational experience of your conversion process, and will hopefully give you happy memories that you will remember for ever.

Sooner or later the Beth Din will suggest that you are ready now to begin what might be called the run-up to the end, although it can be quite a slow and protracted run-up. In particular, it will in most cases be suggested that you move in with a family for a period of time – which can be as short as six months, but is sometimes a year or longer – so as to obtain intensive experience of actual Jewish practice.

Clearly, as an educational opportunity it is hard to imagine anything more effective than living with a family and observing every changing facet of the Jewish year from their perspective. You can learn much about the Jewish laws of kashrus from books – but by helping to prepare meals in a family kitchen you will learn more in a short time than you could ever learn in any other way. In other aspects of Jewish ritual, while working with a tutor you have to keep a mental or written list of questions that arise during the week to ask when you next have a session: and the opportunities for going through the list may be limited, as there is so much else to get through. But when you live with a family you will have an opportunity to ask whatever you like more or less whenever you like; and you will find that your questions multiply with the opportunity to have them answered promptly.

So why is it that this unique learning experience is so often talked about amongst prospective converts as though it were a dread ordeal to be avoided at all costs or suffered for as short a time as possible as the worst part of the price to be paid for successful conversion?

There are a few reasons for this. One is financial, which I discuss later under Question 10. The two other main objections regularly advanced to undergoing the process of moving in with a family are: (a) that it is enormously disruptive of a person's "regular" routine; and (b) that it is unnecessary, it being possible to learn practical aspects of Jewish observance by mixing socially with other members of the local synagogue and spending time in their houses.

On the first objection, it is quite true that it is enormously disruptive to ask a person to leave their own home and spend months in someone else's. Particularly for people who left their parents' home some time ago and have established their own domestic routine, probably based around their professional commitments, it is asking a great deal. But conversion is a disruptive process: if someone is genuinely committed to disrupting their entire way of life and to entering into a close spiritual bond with the Jewish community, the inconvenience of moving house for a few months is likely to be insignificant compared to the other readjustments required of them in the short, medium and long-terms. Again, someone genuinely anxious to acquire as much knowledge of Jewish practice as possible could be expected to jump at the chance of sharing the daily lives of experienced practitioners.

As to the second objection, it is true that more or less from the first day when the prospective convert pushed a tentative and nervous head around the door of his or her local synagogue they will probably have been overwhelmed with advice and information from all sides. If they have managed to locate a genuinely orthodox synagogue, in particular, they will have found, once accepted as established, that any attempt to turn services into an occasion for communication with God will have been obliterated by people from all sides of the synagogue telling them what to do, what not to do, what matters, what does not matter, and generally contradicting each other ten to the dozen about all matters liturgical and ritual.

And here is the problem: if one could assume that the prospective convert will have been left alone and cold-shouldered from the beginning, it might be possible to dispense with much of the services of tutor and host family, and rely on books alone until a relatively late stage. But the first and hardest job of the tutor is to discover and dispel the mass of mis-information which the candidate will have acquired, mostly from people trying to be helpful. (Interestingly, when the tutor is dealing with the "Jewish half" of a marriage-inspired regularisation case, the problem is even worse – most Jews have spent their lives acquiring the most surprising misconceptions of Jewish belief and practice.)

In the same way the most pressing reason for moving in with a family whose understanding of religious practice is tolerably sound is to dispel all the false impressions that will have been acquired from others. Early on in the process the prospective convert will have noticed that as soon as his or her tutor teaches the laws about a particular matter, the next visit to the local synagogue will show that most of the congregants have not the foggiest idea what they are doing, and that those who are most vocal in laying down the law about matters of observance are particularly unlikely to know anything about them. So it is only by moving in with a family that the candidate can tap a single source of reliable information, to remove all the misinformation already acquired and eventually replace it with correct information.

Moving in with a family may also be the candidate's first real opportunity to experience life in a vibrant orthodox community. Unless he or she has happened to have been living all along in or near one of the centres of orthodox Jewish life, this may be one of the most important benefits of this stage of the conversion process: in particular, it may be the first opportunity to observe how an orthodox community operates and to compare and contrast different styles and traditions of religious observance. After the conversion is complete the convert will have to make a number of choices of a kind that many

Jews never have to make, since he or she is unable to rely on the family traditions that ideally dictate most of a person's religious habits and customs; exposure to a large number of different approaches to different aspects of religious life is the best preparation that a convert can have for making these choices.

So in almost all cases there is no legitimate objection (subject to the later discussion about finances) to moving in with a family, and a great deal to be gained from the experience. And my observations over the years suggest that in almost all (but not quite all) cases, an objection to moving in with a family is a reliable indication that a person is less than serious about his or her commitment to changing their lifestyle and joining the orthodox Jewish community.

Having said which, every case is unique, and the candidate will find the Dayonim happy to discuss whether moving in with a family is appropriate. Mere practical inconvenience is, however, unlikely to be considered a sufficient reason for omitting this critical and valuable step in the process.

After a period of staying with a family, at one of the regular six-monthly interviews with the Beth Din it will be agreed by all that the candidate is ready to complete the process. The Beth Din will set a date and time for the candidate to take the final step, immersion in a mikveh. There are mikvaot in London, Manchester and a few other towns in the United Kingdom. The candidate will attend an appointment at a mikveh with three Dayonim, who will attest to the completion of this final step in the process. The candidate emerges from the mikveh having instantaneously, completely and irrevocably changed his or her status, from non-Jew to Jew.

There is nothing frightening or uncomfortable about the mikveh appointment: mikvaot nowadays are clean and warm, and your appointment will be at a time during the day when nobody else is using the mikveh. So you can be assured of privacy and comfort. Normally, married ladies use the mikveh once a month at night and most men do not use it at all, except for a visit once a year before Yom Kippur. The mikveh is simply a pool which consists of rain water originally, although it will have been topped up with mains water since it was first filled. Your tutor will have prepared you for some of the associations of purity and dedication connected with the mikveh, and the visit can be an emotional and spiritually satisfying experience, particularly coming as the culmination of many months of commitment and preparation.

Before the mikveh appointment, a male candidate will have to attend to bris miloh (see Question 12).

There is one other small matter requiring to be taken care of the at the final stages, which can be overlooked. You could regard it as the crowning oddity of what is overall an odd introduction to a decidedly odd religion. Metal and glass vessels and utensils used for food require to be dipped in a mikveh before being used, when a Jew acquires them from a non-Jew. This is nothing to do with kashrus: a knife may have been used only for kosher food, or never used at all, but on acquisition by a Jew from a non-Jew it requires immersion in a mikveh. So far so inexplicable: but it gets more peculiar still – on the completion of the conversion process the convert becomes as a matter of Jewish law a new person, with a legal personality distinct from his or her former identity. The result is that property owned by the convert both immediately before conversion and immediately after it, has passed from a non-Jewish owner to a Jewish owner, and requires immersion! A convert will have been keeping the laws of kashrus at home for some time before conversion, so there should be no need to undertake any of the processes required to render kosher utensils that have been used for non-kosher food: that being so, it is easy to forget that there is a requirement to have all the utensils immersed, and not every tutor remembers to remind the convert helpfully in advance.

Bris Miloh, mikveh and that's it! Such a brief and low-key culmination to months and years of preparation. No formal celebrations or elaborate rituals of any kind. A convert may choose to make a celebratory meal to mark his or her successful conversion, but there is no requirement to do so and most do nothing at all in this way or only something small and discreet.

So the convert comes out of the mikveh, says goodbye to the Dayonim and, so to speak, walks off entirely alone. From a life of daily contact with his or her host family, weekly sessions with the tutor and regular meetings with the Dayonim, the convert is suddenly cast upon his or her own resources, so far as the Rabbinic establishment is concerned. Hopefully, the local Rabbi and community will by now be providing a supportive and welcoming environment: but that is not to be depended on, since it varies so much according to the disposition of the community and the character and resources of the Rabbi.

The absence of a formal after-sales service is a real issue for many converts, and intimately associated with some of their other social problems discussed in Question 18. Although the London Beth Din does offer some kind of follow-up meeting after a few months, and other Botei

Din hopefully do at least as much and may possibly do more, it seems to me that the establishment should acknowledge a formal responsibility to support and assist those who have overcome so many obstacles and difficulties in order to comply with the established procedures and become part of us.

One final word on how to handle the process. It is important and in everybody's interests to be absolutely open and honest with the Dayonim from the start. I have already given the example that concealing the presence of a Jewish boyfriend or girlfriend is likely only to lead to the whole process being delayed once their presence emerges, since they will become part of the process and will have to be assigned a tutor (and normally prove slower and more difficult to teach than the non-Jewish partner). Even worse than that, if the candidate succeeded in keeping an intended marriage hidden from the Dayonim and it only emerged after the process was completed, there is the terrible prospect of doubts being cast later about the original sincerity of the conversion, and its authenticity being called into question. Whereas if the Dayonim know what they are dealing with from the beginning, they can find the appropriate way of dealing with it. As will be apparent from earlier Questions, there is absolutely (although possibly surprisingly) no bar to conversions that are undertaken with a view to marriage; but they need to be approached in that light from the start. This goes too for any other matter that the candidate may find embarrassing to mention to the Beth Din: best get it over with early.

So honesty is the candidate's best policy: but at the same time do not be too hard on yourself. One Jewish partner of a gerus candidate turned up at the Beth Din to tell the Dayonim that he was absolutely committed to living an observant lifestyle and doing anything and everything that they or his very committed fiancée wanted: but he thought they ought to know that he did not believe in God. The Dayan concerned was rather taken aback at this and made a series of rather discouraging noises, so much so that the fiancée took fright, ditched the partner and completed the process solo (and later married a Satmar Chossid). The tragic part of this is that it was apparent to most that the person really did believe in God – at least as much or more as most observant Jews – but was so distrustful of his own understanding that he mistook the kind of doubts and disquiets, without which a person cannot really be said to be searching for God as is required by the Torah, as proof of a fundamental lack of belief. So the message is – be honest, but be circumspect!

Question 7 – How does the process work in America?

The main difference between the process confronting a prospective convert in America and the process in the United Kingdom is that in America there is no single orthodox Rabbinic body to which one can obviously turn for a conversion that will satisfy everybody.

Although nominally local, the London Beth Din satisfies for all practical purposes the requirements of a single co-ordinated national conversion authority for the whole of the United Kingdom; while it is an institution principally serving the "middle of the road" United Synagogue modern orthodoxy, in conversion matters its actions will satisfy both the right-wing Union of Orthodox Hebrew Congregations (based primarily in Stamford Hill) and the left-wing progressive movements. There is no single equivalent in America. There are, however, a number of Rabbinic organisations that may serve an equivalent function for all the circles in which a person is likely to wish to function following conversion, and whose authority is sufficiently recognised by most others to enable a convert and his or her family to lead a reasonably unrestricted Jewish life.

So how should an American convert go about starting the process? Probably in the same way as a British convert, so far as the first step is concerned: he or she should make contact with the most local congregation that claims to be orthodox. Once there, they can inquire of the Rabbi which process is most likely to command widespread acceptance for their purposes and proceed according to his (if a her, try again!) advice. But they should proceed with caution; keeping their eyes open as they make progress to see how wide a section of Jewry they are brought into contact with, and taking advice from various Jews whom they encounter.

As in so many other matters, the Lubavitch organisation may be indispensible here: while I would not advise anybody to convert under Lubavitch auspices (and I doubt that they officially provide such a service anywhere in the world) I would strongly encourage anyone to take advice from a local Lubavitch Rabbi as to where to go to pursue a conversion course: they would direct a prospective candidate only to organisations of unimpeachable religious integrity and authority.

The most important pitfall to avoid is that of converting under the personal aegis of any single Rabbi, however apparently prestigious or reputable. No responsible Rabbi will undertake to do more than to introduce a person to a competent Beth Din or Rabbinic organisation and, possibly, thereafter to provide tutoring services in support of a programme supervised by that organisation. Anyone who purports to handle the entire process himself, providing tutoring himself or through a relation or subordinate, and providing what is essentially a personal certificate of conversion, is a fraud.

Question 8 – How does the process work in Israel?

Israel has almost the opposite problem to that of America. There is one obvious central Rabbinic system that handles conversions – the national Rabbinate – and all a prospective candidate has to do is to look up the local office of the Rabbinate in the telephone book. But the problem is that it is too easy in some ways to be processed by the Israeli system, with the result that a person may comply with all its requirements but emerge with a status that, although accepted as valid throughout Israel for most or all official purposes, may not always be good enough for the convert or his or her family for all religious purposes, particularly outside Israel.

This is just one reflection of a fundamental issue about religious practice in Israel, that can be described by reference to the philosophical difference between the Mizrachi or "centrist" orthodoxy and the Chareidi or "ultra-orthodox" communities. The best explanation I ever heard of this difference was offered by someone taking me round an orthodox kibbutz shortly before a Sabbatical year, when the members of the kibbutz were having to decide whether they would rely on the nominal sale of the whole land by the Chief Rabbinate of Israel or whether they would make special arrangements. In essence, he said, everyone agrees that in purely theoretical halachic terms it is preferable to make special arrangements, and this is what the one or two ultra-orthodox kibbutzim do; but the point is that for various reasons (which I will not elaborate because this is a book about conversion and not the Sabbatical year) it is not practicable for the whole of the Israeli agricultural system to make individual arrangements, and therefore if one wants a system that is reasonably practicable to operate on a nation-wide basis, the nominal sale is the only sensible way forward.

Essentially the same thought process applies to conversion. Everyone agrees that the best approach is to have each candidate carefully schooled by a Beth Din-appointed tutor for a period of at least a couple of years, interspersed with individual meetings with the Dayonim, and with his or her personal progress being tracked and supported carefully in a number of ways. And that is a practical proposition in the United Kingdom, where the London Beth Din may encounter perhaps fifty or a hundred new cases of prospective conversion each year, many of which will not proceed beyond the opening stages. But it is not practicable if you have, for example, twenty thousand people arriving in Israel from Russia in one year with at best doubtful Jewish status requiring to be processed for conversion as part of what for everybody's sake needs to be a swift and efficient absorption into Israeli society.

So the system as applied by the Israeli Rabbinate requires to be capable of processing thousands of times the numbers for which the British system is designed. And there is another factor as well: in order to lead a Jewish religious life in Britain, even in North West London or one of the other centres of Jewish life, a person needs a good grasp of practical halachah to deal with the kashrus and other issues that arise in the course of a normal week. That is much less true for a person who proposes to live in a religious area in an Israeli town: without being the most dedicated and self-disciplined convert of all time, and without being noticeably more knowledgeable in halachah than most nominally orthodox Jews, he or she will be carried along the paths of an observant life merely by taking part in the community. The schools will provide their children with an orthodox Jewish education, often vastly superior to that given to the children of even the highly committed Jews here in the United Kingdom; the shops will in general sell only kosher produce, and someone wanting to buy something that is not kosher would have to go to a specialist shop for it if it were available at all – the precise reverse of the situation in the United Kingdom; and daily services will be available at about thirty seconds walk and will be attended as a matter of routine by most people.

As a result, the Israeli Rabbinate are likely to feel able to take on trust to a considerable extent the future religious life of a convert who plans to live in an orthodox area, something that the British Rabbinate could not responsibly do.

This is good and bad. It is good because it enables a genuinely committed convert to complete the process in Israel with considerably less difficulty, and cost, than is possible for British candidates. But it is bad because the scope for abuse is much greater – it being possible to slip through the system without any genuine intention to accept the requirements of a Torah lifestyle; the result of that is that a Rabbinate conversion certificate will not necessarily be accepted throughout the world – or even throughout Israeli society – as sufficient evidence in itself of a genuine conversion.

This enables us to explain one of the recent sources of controversy about conversion, Israeli converts not being accepted as Jewish on arrival in the United Kingdom. In one case there was even a certificate of conversion issued by the Israeli Rabbinate and marked as being valid only in Israel, something which caused bewilderment and controversy in the Jewish media in the United Kingdom. In other cases, without any express purported territorial limitation an Israeli certificate has apparently been rejected by the British Dayonim.

The point is that someone who was processed by the Israeli Rabbinate without any special attention is taking the benefit of, in effect, a presumption that he or she intends to live a Torah life, a presumption supported by their choice of an orthodox community for their future life. But the presumption is rebuttable. As we have said above, a lapse of religious commitment after conversion does not invalidate a conversion: once Jewish, always Jewish. But a lack of evidence that a person ever lived a Torah lifestyle may rebut the presumption on the basis of which their conversion was accepted originally: according to everyone, a genuine acceptance of Torah law is a requisite of a valid conversion – the only difference is the standard of evidence that will be relied upon in respect of that acceptance at the outset. If it emerges that the convert never spent any period of his or her life living an observant lifestyle, even for the few months or years immediately following the conversion process, the presumption of genuine intent will be rebutted and, in effect, the conversion will be regarded as never having been valid, owing to the lack of any real commitment to orthodox Judaism on the part of the convert. In cases of this kind the person will be treated as non-Jewish, and children will be treated as taking their status accordingly, depending on whether the converted person was the mother or the father.

There is a separate issue about the many thousands of conversions conducted in Israel under the auspices of Rabbi Druckman, as to which doubt has been cast, then un-cast and then cast again by a series of pronouncements by various religious authorities and secular courts. This is a matter of high religious politics (or low, would perhaps be the better adjective) and the situation is liable to change by reference to issues of religious and political power that have nothing to do with conversion itself or indeed religion at all. So I prefer not to comment much here on the issue, not knowing enough about the politics involved. I have a hope that it will "blow over" in time, and that no doubt will be raised about the validity of these conversions when it comes to official religious status; and those people who may be inclined to continue to sneer at individual products of these conversions will be the kind of people who will find other reasons for sneering at, and casting doubt about, any cases that do not conform to their own social stereotypes and norms.

A later edition of this book may be able to say more about the Rabbi Druckman issue, and will hopefully be able to consign it to a historical footnote as a bombshell that smoked a lot at one stage but never exploded. My latest information at the time of writing, having inquired from those with knowledge of the process in Israel, is that although the doubts about Rabbi Druckman's conversions will probably be allowed to fade in time, much is being done to delay the process so far as possible; this is entirely a political dispute, but the victims are not politicians but the increasing numbers of innocent individuals who converted in good faith, and who, or whose children, are now facing agonising delays and uncertainties when it comes to processing marriages or other matters.

Question 9 – What are the basic skills a candidate needs to master?

Because it would be a shame if this book were entirely without practical value for prospective converts, the answer to this Question borders on something approaching useful advice.

The laws appertaining to Jewish ritual can be mastered in anything between three months and seventy years. A reasonably intelligent person who sets out to study intensively with the assistance of an experienced tutor can in three months assimilate enough of the basic laws of religious ritual to know more than most of the people who have been nominally observant for twenty or thirty years of their lives. On the other hand, ask a scholar who has been learning in yeshivah for, say, thirty or forty years a question about a detail of the laws of Shabbos and he is quite likely to say that he has never made much of a study of that area of halachah and to recommend you to ask someone else, who is likely to say the same and again redirect you; finally you will arrive either at someone who admits to being an expert in the laws of Shabbos (in which case he is probably no such thing and will probably give you the wrong answer) or to someone whom everyone assures you is not to be taken seriously when he protests that he is no expert. Jewish law is like that: the basics are easily learned, but the more you learn of the detail the more you realise how little you understand of even the basics.

A prospective candidate for conversion will be relieved to learn that he or she is not expected to study for forty years before being considered sufficiently knowledgeable in practical halachah to be admitted as part of the community. On the other hand, a three month course is generally thought insufficient (although in one extreme case, for various compelling reasons of a pressing social nature, I was instructed to teach a prospective convert as much as we could cover in three months and leave it at that). Precisely where to draw the line between three months and forty years is always difficult to know, and depends as much in practice on the family and social circumstances of the candidate as on anything else.

The understanding is that it matters relatively little where one draws the line for conversion, because a candidate who converts with serious intentions of joining the orthodox community will join the rest of us in a continuing programme of study of Jewish law, so that until the day one dies one is discovering more and more about what one ought to have been doing since the day one was born. It is not unusual for a study group about the laws of blessings, for example, to conclude that both the Rabbi giving it and everyone attending it have been making the wrong blessing on a particular food throughout their lives; but it does not seem to perturb anyone – on the contrary, we congratulate ourselves on our enhanced knowledge and move on (sometimes pausing to write a smug letter to one of the orthodox Jewish newspapers to inform our co-religionists that we are sure they must have been aware of the fact that we have only just discovered ... and so on and so forth).

Having said all that, there are certain basic skills that are likely to be required for all candidates for conversion. Put another way, a person who has been permitted to complete the course without mastering the following skills can be reasonably sure that his or her conversion has not been handled by a responsible Beth Din and is therefore at risk of not being generally accepted as valid.

> Knowledge by heart of the basic blessings before eating and drinking

> Ability to recite fluently from a siddur (prayer book) the three blessings after eating and drinking

> Knowledge by heart of the five or so most common blessings on other events

Ability to recite fluently from a siddur the morning blessings and the *Shema Yisroel* prayer

For men, ability to put on tefilin (phylacteries – small leather boxes containing scriptural passages, bound loosely onto the arm and head with leather straps during morning prayers)

Knowledge of the central rituals and customs practiced in the Jewish home on Shabbos and Yom Tov

Knowledge of the basic rules of kashrus – what may not be eaten, separation of milk and meat, and so on

There are a number of other minor issues that will be covered in any competent conversion course: but they are all incidental and second-order in practice.

It will be seen that some familiarity with written Hebrew, enough to recite fluently the most common prayers, will be required. This should not be a cause for concern. Hebrew is probably the easiest language in the world to learn to read: its essentially phonetic combination of consonants and vowel notations can be mastered by an adult of moderate intelligence easily in ten one-hour lessons, following which practice will speedily make perfect. Someone with serious language difficulties would not be required to learn Hebrew at all: for anyone else, it should be the easiest part of the process. Even learning to translate Hebrew is an easier task than for many languages – all Hebrew words derive from a three-letter root with a variety of prefixes and suffixes, which show much less irregularity than does, for example, English: it is pleasing how few roots there are or, to put it another way, how large a proportion of Hebrew words the acquisition of a handful of the commonest roots enables you to understand.

The only other essential skill of the Jewish religion which ought to be, but will not be, taught as part of the conversion course is the ability to make jokes that show a total lack of deference to God, to other Jews or to oneself. In reality, there is only one Jewish joke, of which all others are mutant derivates. Here it is—

> A grandmother was taking her grandson for a walk along the seashore. He had been dressed up specially for the occasion, as befitted so important a fashion accessory as a walking grandson. He wore a navy blue sailor suit, with a smart blue and white cap in strict nautical fashion.

Suddenly, a freak wave blows up from out in the ocean, surges onto the shore, lifts up the grandson and hurls him far out to sea. The grandmother falls on her knees distraught and wails an instant prayer from the heart to the Lord of Creation.

> "Dear God – if I have ever earned any merit by anything I have done in my life, I willingly give up every merit I have earned in Your eyes if you will only restore my grandson to me."

She gazes desperately out to sea, and within seconds observes a small wave begin to mount higher and higher: it surges onto the shore, deposits her grandson at her feet and rushes back into the ocean.

The grandmother looks down at the child at her feet; dishevelled and discomposed, his little sailor suit muddy and tattered, but clearly alive and well. She casts her eyes up to the Heavens and says, in a complaining voice—

> "He had a cap …"

Question 10 – How much does conversion cost?

This is an important question, which affects or is affected by some of the most problematic issues surrounding conversion today.

As will have been seen, strictly speaking there is no reason why conversion should cost anybody anything at all. The actual costs of the occasional appointment with the Beth Din and a single mikveh appointment are so small that they could either be absorbed into the community's budget or be passed on to the convert at an insignificant figure.

The reality is that the incidental but unavoidable costs of conversion are very considerable, and there is a tendency on the part of the establishment to regard the requirement to spend significant sums of money as one of the ways by which the sincerity and commitment of prospective converts can be assessed.

There is, of course, something in this: it is true that spending money can sometimes focus the mind in a way that other things do not. It is also true that someone toying with the idea of becoming Jewish might be sufficiently serious to be prepared to give up considerable amounts of time to learning about the religion without being very seriously committed – particularly if they have not too many other calls upon their time – but might think again if they were asked to choose to allocate a significant proportion of their disposable income to the process.

My main objection to the use of money as a test of sincerity is that although it could in some cases be an indication, there are many other ways of establishing a person's sincerity, while the use of money as a test creates two specific and troubling dangers that the other tests would not. The first danger is that certain people whose spiritual commitment is real but whose means are slight will feel excluded from the process by the simple inability to "pay their way": a prospective convert of great humility – and all the "real" cases fall into this category – may doubt both his or her own sincerity and his or her own importance too much to prevail upon others to waive charges, and may fall regretfully away from the process at an early stage without even daring to mention to the Beth Din or anyone else that their decision not to pursue the process any further is essentially financial. I am intensely troubled by the idea that some of the most potentially beneficial additions to our community may have been deterred at an early stage – perhaps before they had a chance to determine or appreciate their own intensity of interest – by demands for money which they simply did not have.

The second danger is that by the introduction of charges we confuse our own motives and roles in relation to the process of conversion and expose ourselves to the charge – whether from others or from our own conscience – that our involvement in the process is essentially mercenary. More specifically, we create the possibility of conflicts of interest and other potential financial problems.

I have sometimes had it put to me that in relation to tutoring in particular it is important to charge on the grounds that people value what they pay for more than what they are given free. Again, there is something in that. But there is a counter-argument: in the world today there is very little that is not for sale, and people with money can come to feel that money is the most important thing in life simply because it is capable of buying them everything they desire. There is no product, service, skill or source of knowledge that cannot be placed at their disposal if they are prepared to pay someone for it.

The danger is that Torah knowledge can therefore come to be seen as a commodity like any other. If I want to learn Chinese, I go to a language school and pay for lessons; and the more I am prepared to pay, the better the tuition that I am likely to find or that I am entitled to expect and demand. It can be an intensely powerful lesson for a person to discover that the Torah is not for sale – that the most reliable guardians of Torah knowledge are not prepared to part with it for money, but are happy to give it free of charge to those whom they think proper recipients. To know that the few most influential Torah scholars of each generation devote their energy not to building reputations and fortunes but to acquiring more knowledge for its own sake, and that they will not be induced by the offer of mere money to interrupt their learning in order to teach, could be a powerful inspiration to a prospective convert, particularly to one who inhabits a professional or social world in which money and the acquisition of money are both the primary motivating factors and the ultimate tests of success and personal worth. It is not likely, of course, that a prospective convert can expect to have much or any exposure to these rare Torah giants at an early stage in the process: but if the tutors, who in a small way represent the Torah world to the candidate for conversion until he or she progresses further, can set an example of not appearing to be motivated primarily by money, we can at least start the education as we hope it will continue.

Against that must be balanced the importance of prospective converts being taught reliably and effectively, which as a general rule requires qualified tutors with both a sufficiency of knowledge and at least an aptitude for, and preferably a training in, teaching. And professional teachers need to eat, as do their families.

The result of these conflicting considerations is something of a conundrum, which does not permit of a single obvious solution. In the final analysis, I see no practicable alternative to the use for the most part of paid tutors to teach prospective converts; and paid hosts when they come to that part of their education that requires them to move in with families. But I would put into place two changes to the present system in the United Kingdom that would, I think, do much to prevent money from becoming a corrupting influence in the purity of the conversion process as a whole.

First, I would formalise arrangements for the provision of tutors and hosts for those who simply cannot properly be expected to finance the arrangements themselves. Rather than expect professional tutors or host families to jeopardise their own financial situations out of compassion by lowering or waiving their charges, and rather than having the ability to pay featuring as part of the reasoning in determining the allocation of tutors to candidates or families, I would prefer to see established a formal fund, administered by the Beth Din, for the payment of the charges of tutors and host families for candidates who have been accepted onto the programme and whose finances are such as to require support. I would encourage charitable donations to this fund in the same way as for other funds; but I would in particular encourage tutors and host families to consider donating to this fund at least that part of their income from candidates that they are halachically obliged to set aside for charitable purposes; and I would also encourage successful candidates, when they have completed the process and their decision whether or not to donate could not be thought to influence their progress, to consider making a donation to the fund.

Secondly, I would confront the necessity of candidates' paying for much of the process and make more of the importance of ensuring that they receive value for money. There should be a formal system by which candidates, even while the process is continuing, are actively encouraged to report on the quality of the education that they are receiving, at the same time as tutors are being encouraged to report on the quality of the learning. The Beth Din should inspect the accommodation provided by host families and satisfy themselves that candidates are being well served. Anecdotal experience leads me to expect that both for tutors and for hosts the reports of candidates will be overwhelmingly positive, and that they will in general feel that they are receiving an excellent and cost-effective service:

but at present they feel inhibited from expressing any opinion on it in case it should somehow "count against them", and this compounds the injustice of the few cases in which the candidate is not receiving fair value for his or her money.

Finally, and looking abroad from the United Kingdom, I would encourage a little more publicity to be given to the fact that certain unscrupulous individuals seek to profiteer out of the conversion process, and exploit prospective converts for financial gain in a number of ways. To give two examples, one person in a "marriage case" told me that he had been told by a certain group of apparently respectable, and certainly well-reputed, Rabbis operating from the United Kingdom, that it was not unlikely that he did in fact have Jewish ancestors a few generations back, and that the lengthy and costly process of conversion through the London Beth Din could perhaps be circumvented by a little genealogical research which would, however, cost a certain amount of money upfront to undertake…!

In another case, a couple who wanted to get married and one of whom was the product of a Reform conversion were induced to part with a considerable amount of money by way of an ostensibly charitable donation to the institutions run by a prominent Rabbi outside the United Kingdom, who thereupon undertook to convert the non-Jewish partner in a matter of a few weeks and subsequently to perform a Jewish marriage ceremony himself which he assured them would be under the Israeli Rabbinate and would therefore command international authority: the conversion process was in fact nugatory, the marriage was performed in Israel but under the Rabbi's personal auspices and without receiving Israeli Rabbinate recognition (a fact that the couple discovered only later); and since the couple did not know nearly enough to run an orthodox Jewish home together the conversion was perforce not recognised in any of the mainstream Jewish communities internationally.

People who want to convert, and even more so people who "need" to convert for marriage or other status reasons, are a vulnerable group and they are open to exploitation in a number of ways. The Jewish community needs to accept it as an obligation to protect these people from being taken advantage of, and to use publicity or other methods to try to prevent the unscrupulous from exploiting them.

These considerations apart, the costs associated with the conversion process vary according to circumstances; but a candidate should allow something in the region of £30 to £50 per session of tutoring, which might be weekly over a period of anything from one to three years; and a market rate for board and lodging at any host family that he or she moves into; plus an amount for the purchase of new kosher utensils and a total of a few hundred pounds for various books and other religious items. In the case of a male candidate, in particular, he will need at some point to buy a pair of tefilin; these cost anything from a couple of hundred pounds to many hundred, depending on what quality he wants to have and can afford. In a case where the candidate already has a Jewish boyfriend or girlfriend, the boyfriend or girlfriend will also have to study with a tutor and may have to buy tefilin and other religious articles (even someone who already has a pair of tefilin is likely to find that they are no longer kosher, having worn over the years, or perhaps that they were never of a sufficient standard of kashrus).

Putting it all together, the combined cost of the process is likely to amount to a few thousand pounds. In a case where the candidate simply cannot afford the costs, the Beth Din or local community will doubtless do what they can to help, and a candidate should certainly not be reluctant to explain his or her financial circumstances where necessary. But as I say above, that is not the whole answers; although there is much communal kindness that can be drawn upon if necessary, the system should not be designed in such a way as to burden people unnecessarily.

Question 11 – How long does the process take?

This is one of the first questions that I am generally asked by someone who comes to me to be tutored for conversion, despite the fact that they have presumably already asked the Beth Din the same question. The answer that I can give them is no more precise than that which they have already presumably been given by the Beth Din: the process must be expected to take years from start to finish, but how many years is impossible to predict.

Strictly speaking, there is no reason why the process should take long at all. The Talmud (Yevomos 47) suggests that at a time when the Jews are generally persecuted, all one needs to do is remind the prospective convert that he or she stands to gain nothing but trouble by converting: if they reply that they aware of this and still account it a privilege for they hardly believe themselves worthy, we can accept them immediately, and should do so after teaching them only the basics of Jewish belief and practice. In other words, in a case where the sincerity of the candidate is beyond any doubt, acceptance can be a very short process.

This principle certainly influences the way in which converts are handled today. Where there is an obvious practical motivation for wanting to convert – the most obvious example being a prospective marriage – the imposition of an element of delay is one of the most obvious and effective ways of determining whether the desire to convert is entirely subordinate to and contingent upon the marriage or whether it is a sincere commitment to undertaking to live according to the Torah. And prospective converts are certainly warned at the outset of the process that anything akin to impatience will not only fail to expedite their case but may introduce the kind of doubt about their sincerity that could delay it or even be fatal to the possibility of a successful conclusion.

In reality, however, there are all kinds of reason why it is important for everyone to get the process of conversion over as quickly as possible. Prospective converts frequently have considerable reason for a desire for haste on their side: in the most common case, where a particular marriage is in view, the families are generally keen to proceed with the marriage as soon as is reasonably possible. In particular, there are obvious and compelling reasons why many of the women involved in conversion cases for marriage are anxious not to delay even a month longer than is strictly necessary: it seems to be common for "marriage cases" for conversion to involve women in their early or mid-thirties, and a sometimes completely unexpected need to undertake a lengthy conversion process before the marriage can take place introduces a very considerable emotional strain, founded on well-known and distinctly uncomfortable medical facts.

But even where there is no particular reason for hurry on the part of the prospective convert or anyone else who is, so to speak, awaiting the result, contrary to popular perception the Beth Din themselves are most unwilling that the process should last longer than necessary. The status of conversion-candidate is an equivocal one which is uncomfortable both for the candidate and also for the community as a whole: it is inevitable and desirable that the candidate should participate in the religious and social life of the community while learning how to live as an orthodox Jew, but his or her involvement is obviously subject to limitations and inhibitions while their status is not yet resolved. It can cause the candidate considerable embarrassment to have to inform, for example, every Shabbos host that he or she is not Jewish (for purposes of avoiding difficulties in relation to wine, for example, or in order to avoid being counted unwittingly for the three Jewish men required for a particular form of grace after meals). And, perhaps more importantly, there is the possibility that people will see the candidate in synagogue or in the community and, not knowing that they are not yet Jewish, think of or even propose matrimonial possibilities for them, and perhaps mention their possible suitability to the other party that they have in mind, with a risk of creating embarrassment at the least or the serious disappointment of false expectations. For all these and other reasons, it is desirable that the process should be concluded as quickly as possible.

What is possible, however, is simply a question of how long it takes to impart the necessary knowledge and to establish the necessary sincerity of intention, to be sure that the convert once fully "processed" will lead a fully Jewish life. The problem is that realistically this can take a number of years, and very often the cases which one might think should be easiest and quickest to complete (and who come to the Beth Din with the expectation that this will be the case) are the ones that require the most attention and the lengthiest education. In particular, it is generally assumed that "regularisation cases", since they have been exposed to Jewish life for many years and in some cases have lived for the whole of their lives as part of a family or community with ostensible orthodox affiliations, will be relatively easy to process, the candidate starting from an advantageous position of knowledge as compared to a "real" non-Jew from outside the community. The reality is certainly not so; indeed, it is almost the reverse. Any tutor of "regularisation" candidates for conversion or Jewish partners of a candidate knows that the first part of process is not one of education but of debriefing; disabusing them of all the partial knowledge and misunderstandings that they have been taught in their childhood or acquired from observation of their peers. The level of knowledge of basic Jewish law in even the orthodox community is for the most part bewilderingly low: people "get by" by doing what they and their families have done in the past, often based on faulty observation of others or failure to appreciate the significance of different circumstances. The result is that when required to demonstrate basic systematic knowledge or understanding of ritual law most people fall woefully short of a standard at which the Dayonim are likely to be convinced that they have the ability – leaving inclination aside – to lead a life of reasonably exacting halachic observance without significant study, which will generally need to begin with unlearning the half-knowledge so far acquired.

As a rough rule of thumb, from a standing start – that is to say coming to the community from the outside and without any significant knowledge of Jewish practice or belief – it is unrealistic to expect to complete the process in less than three years; and considerably more than that might be required. If there is no reason for particular hurry – which is principally a question of the age and gender of the candidate – five years is probably a more realistic target for a person of average intelligence and memory at the beginning. If there is reason for hurry, a person of exceptional intelligence and with an unusually quick and retentive memory might hope – but not reliably expect – to start and complete the entire process within about two years. For someone starting with a background of exposure to the Jewish community, the process may be shorter: but, for the reasons given above, it may not be significantly shorter, because simple exposure to Jewish practice in the synagogue and even at home rarely provides the kind of thorough knowledge required by someone setting out to live a rigorously self-disciplined orthodox Jewish life. Again, between one and two years might be an ambitious but not entirely unrealistic target.

Of course, many people will offer to provide a conversion in considerably less than this kind of period. Anyone can call himself "Rabbi X"; and any three Rabbis X, Y and Z can constitute themselves a Beth Din, shove up a brass plate and start issuing certificates of conversion. The question is whether the certificate will be worth the paper on which it is printed; which depends on how many people other than Rabbis X, Y and Z will regard it as authoritative. More will be said elsewhere in this book about how to choose an appropriate Beth Din; but for the purposes of this Question suffice it to say that anyone holding out serious hopes of achieving a conversion in less than a year should be avoided at all costs, unless there are very significant reasons why faster progress can be expected and justified in the special circumstances of the case.

Question 12 – Will I need to be circumcised?

Circumcision is a requisite for all Jewish boys and men. Unlike much of the Jewish ritual that we practice today, it was commanded before the transmission of the Torah to Moses on Mount Sinai and has been practiced, in an absolutely unchanged form, since the times of Abraham. This alone gives it a sentiment and value that makes the circumcision of a child an emotional experience of bonding him to the unbroken line of ancestral tradition: as such, while mothers find it as traumatic to know that their child is suffering as Abraham himself found it to take his son Isaac to the altar, there is the same joy at being able to serve God unquestioningly by devotion to His will, as transmitted and cherished through the ages.

The symbolism of the bris miloh is discussed in many places in Rabbinic literature. A central theme is the notion that God sends man into the world in a form that man is then allowed to "improve upon", thereby emphasising the role of the child's parents as partners with God in the act of creation. (The circumcision is performed on the eighth day: which is why the seven first days of creation of the world were by God alone, then came the first Sabbath, and from then on the continuing act of creation and perfection is intended to be a partnership between God and human beings.)

As a male convert to Judaism you will therefore certainly be required to undergo a circumcision, shortly before the completion of the conversion process (and before your immersion in the mikveh, discussed below). When a Jewish boy is circumcised we describe him as entering the Covenant of Abraham our Father. As a convert, you will be described as a son of Abraham our Father, and the bris miloh that you bear will be a direct link, reaching through the centuries, between you and your adopted father Abraham. In the same way that Abraham subjected himself to bris miloh at an advanced age having rejected idolatry and discerned the importance of bris miloh from his unrivalled understanding of God's plan for the world, you too will have travelled a long journey, rejecting a number of cultural values and practices, as a result of which you will set the seal on your hard-won closeness to God by entering into His covenant.

Although the thought of circumcision is bound to be a little daunting, the process itself is not something to be at all troubled about. For a young or middle-aged man in normally robust health, in medical terms it counts as a very minor procedure, hardly even worthy of being described as day-surgery. The Beth Din will recommend a mohel, a man who has been trained in the art of circumcision. Many mohelim are doctors, although by no means all; and some of the most skilful, and the most consulted by other mohelim including doctors, have no general medical qualification themselves. For an adult circumcision, however, I have the impression that it is generally thought sensible to have a doctor perform the procedure, and the Beth Din will probably recommend someone who is both a general medical practitioner and an experienced mohel. I am told by those who have undergone the procedure that it is not at all painful, and gives rise at worst merely to discomfort for a short time.

It is possible that you already had a circumcision when you were a baby: either because your parents belonged to a non-orthodox Jewish community and had you circumcised as a matter of course, or because your parents were part of the considerable portion of the world that regards circumcision as a beneficial medical procedure. In either event, the answer to the question often put as a joke "I can't have another one, can I?" is the surprising "you can and must". Without entering into unnecessary biological details, the bris miloh consists of three parts, of which you will only have had one or two; and it requires to be performed expressly as a religious commandment within the context of orthodox Judaism. Therefore if you had a circumcision when you were a child, a mohel will perform a very minor procedure that involves, in most cases, simply a tiny amount of blood to be drawn – a mere pinprick – in the name of Abraham's covenant with God.

Circumcision is neither required nor permitted for girls or women in Judaism. Why the symbolic requirement for partnership in creation is not applicable to them is a matter about which we can only conjecture, and suggestions abound in Rabbinic literature. I have never found one that satisfied me entirely, so I offer none here. The idea that women are born somehow in a more perfect form than men, requiring no intervention, may have some resonance; but it as likely to offend as to pacify. Of course, women participate in the continuing life-cycle of creation in their own very pronounced way; but why the creative roles of the sexes should be distinct in the way it is, I fear is just one more aspect of the Jewish religion that the convert has to take on trust from those who have inherited the tradition of Torah over the ages.

Question 13 – Which is the best country to convert in?

An interesting question (which is why I asked it): and the answer depends on a number of factors.

Of course, not everyone has a choice: their residence in a particular country is determined by financial or other factors over which they have insufficient control to allow them to leave. And yet, as I have said before, it is bewildering and humbling to see the sacrifices that some converts are prepared to make in order to become Jewish, and some are prepared and even eager to abandon their past life and move wherever they need to go in order to achieve their dream of becoming Jewish: as Ruth says (1:16) "wherever you go, I will go; wherever you stay, I will stay".

Not every country in the world has the facilities to offer a conversion process. For one thing, to complete the process requires the presence of a full Beth Din of three Dayonim, something that many countries do not have. There are two possible approaches to conversion in a country with limited resources: I have encountered converts who were prepared for conversion in New Zealand and who had to wait to complete the process until the visit from Australia of sufficient Rabbis to complete the process. But I have also encountered converts from Amsterdam

– a place with considerable Jewish resources of its own and easy access to reinforcements from elsewhere – who were advised by the local Rabbinate to come to London to undertake the entire process here.

One might think that in this day and age knowledge is available so globally as to make it unnecessary to worry much about where a person goes through the process of preparing for conversion: it could be approached like any other branch of knowledge, with learning being acquired from books and websites, and the candidate could travel to London, Jerusalem or anywhere else for a day or two to complete the final stage, once having convinced the Rabbinic authorities, also by remote correspondence, of his or her readiness. Indeed, there are people who appear to encourage that kind of approach: there is at least one website which offers distance learning for the express purpose of preparation for conversion.

But you cannot learn to be Jewish from a book. You can learn <u>about</u> Judaism from a book, and you can even, in theory, become an expert in certain matters of Jewish law from books. But if you try to learn Jewish practice from a book you will certainly go wrong. The biggest problem is the huge number of Jewish texts that have been translated into English so that they are now apparently accessible to all, whereas the information they contain is only designed for application with care and experience by Rabbis: for example, I was once involved with a Jewish family whose mother was becoming rapidly more observant and was guiding herself by buying and reading all the English works about Jewish law she could lay her hands on – the result was that she was happily imposing on herself and her children prohibitions that no sensible Rabbi in the world would have thought appropriate for her family to absorb at that rate and in that way; and in the process she was seriously risking the sanity and security of her family. So any attempt at serious distance learning of Judaism is doomed to serious failure.

The result is that although it may be possible for a candidate for conversion to begin the early steps of the process by reading basic materials anywhere in the world – I know a convert, now an orthodox Rabbi, who wandered into a library in Glasgow at the age of fifteen and taught himself Hebrew as a gentle preliminary to the process of conversion – once the person is ready to make a definite commitment to the conversion process he or she must make up their mind to moving to a place with a significant Jewish community that can provide the necessary facilities: these include active synagogue communities from whose services and members to learn the realities of daily Jewish observance, and also one or more Rabbis or teachers capable of providing expert and appropriate guidance.

That still leaves an unhelpfully wide choice. Some may be led by particular practical considerations to small but sufficient communities almost anywhere in the world. But for most the choices will resolve themselves into the major Jewish communities world-wide: principally in America or Israel.

Before comparing these it may be worth mentioning that England, and specifically London, should always be considered. The London Beth Din is generally thought to be one of the most demanding in the world in what it requires of converts: that can be seen as an advantage for the prospective convert, not a disadvantage, because its result is that anyone who succeeds in converting in London can rest assured that their conversion will be respected wherever else in the world they may wish to go later.

In choosing between America and Israel, language will be a significant factor for many. Although any proper conversion programme will require the convert to master reading Hebrew fluently – a relatively easy task for most people – none will require him or her to become fluent in modern Hebrew, that not being a relevant religious attainment.   That might seem to indicate America, particularly for anyone for whom mastering a new language is a daunting prospect.

On the other hand, Israel is where all orthodox Jews hope to end up, and we pray three times a day for the reinstatement of a fully Jewish society in Israel, ushering in the Messianic redemption. So if you are uprooting yourself once in order to become Jewish, why not cut out the state of exile and start your Jewish life in the place to which all Jews turn as they pray?

Question 14 – Which Beth Din should I choose?

If you are considering converting in the United Kingdom, you should assume that the London Beth Din is your only sensible choice.

The Manchester Beth Din says the following about conversion on its internet website—

> "The Manchester Beth Din acts in conjunction with the London Beth Din who will ultimately carry out the conversion procedures on the successful applicant. The Manchester Beth Din will conduct the initial interviews and arrange one to one tuition for potential converts. It will monitor progress and advise both the potential convert and the London Beth Din."

That being the case, you will certainly end up dealing with the London Beth Din, and you may in the end find moving to London the most effective way of completing the process. So unless you have strong commercial or other reasons for wishing to live in Manchester and to become part of the community there, you may as well start by opening a file with the London Beth Din, rather than opening a file with the Manchester Beth Din and having it transferred to

London in due course. There is a potential for delay and confusion in the latter approach that it would be as well to avoid.

The Sephardi Beth Din in London appears to take an approach similar to that of the Manchester Beth Din, channelling people in the direction of the London Beth Din or, in appropriate cases, to an authority abroad. The majority community in the United Kingdom come from an Ashkenazi tradition, and there is therefore a presumption that it will be appropriate for anyone converting in the United Kingdom to convert into that tradition and become part of one of the many Ashkenazi communities. But there could of course be exceptions. Obvious exceptions would be a "regularisation" case where the father comes from and is still heavily involved with a Sephardi community or a marriage case where the Jewish partner comes from a Sephardi community; and there could well be others.

Apart from the London Beth Din, or one of these other routes that ends up with the London Beth Din sooner or later, you may find other people, Rabbis or persons purporting to be so, who will offer to "arrange" a conversion for you in one way or another. A common offer is to take you to America, Israel or some other country where a speedy and efficient conversion can be arranged without going through all the troublesome bureaucracy of the London Beth Din and complying with its famously stringent requirements. Provided you are well supplied with money, you will not be short of offers; the more money you have and are prepared to spend, the greater the alacrity that certain people will show to help you, and the more they will promise to make the process speedy and easy. I was even told by one person that a small group of people purporting to be Rabbis, and serving communities as Rabbis, had offered that if money were supplied for genealogical researches abroad, they could probably manage to prove that his non-Jewish fiancée came originally from a Jewish background and had a sufficiently clear maternal lineage to establish her Jewish status.

In relation to all these suggestions and offers the appropriate advice is clear and unequivocal. Unless you have a clear reason for converting abroad – the most obvious being that you intend to live there – you will gain only trouble and confusion by converting anywhere outside the country in which you are presently living.

You may be given clear advice to the contrary. I am aware that there is a theory current in certain communities that the best thing a couple can do where they want to marry and one of them is non-Jewish is to have a civil wedding as fast as possible, here or abroad, and then turn to the London Beth Din and say "we're married now so you may as well make it easy for us". There is an additional theory that even better than this is to go abroad, obtain a quick conversion there, be married under the auspices of an American Rabbi, or under the auspices of the official Israeli Rabbinate in reliance on the American conversion, and then come back home and present the whole thing to the London Beth Din as a fait accompli. The theory is that either of these courses, but particularly the second, makes it impossible in practice for the London Beth Din to do anything other than either recognise the foreign conversion or, at least, facilitate a fast and relatively painless first or second conversion here.

The reality is that the only things gained by either of these courses of action are, first, additional confusion and trouble for everybody and, secondly, the probability of children being born with questionable status that cannot afterwards be entirely remedied. The idea that the London Beth Din will feel obliged to hurry the process up because the couple have jumped the gun is simply false: they will apply precisely the same standards as always in judging whether a couple have a sincere desire to live according to the laws of the Torah, so that the formerly non-Jewish partner can be accepted into the community. A conversion granted abroad – or indeed in the United Kingdom – on the basis of a few weeks' superficial study will be treated for what it is worth: nothing. The couple will in effect have to start again from scratch, undergoing a process which is time-consuming and stressful and not a good accompaniment to the early days of a marriage. Where the non-Jewish partner is the mother, any children born before the process is completed will be born as non-Jews, so far as the Jewish community of the United Kingdom is concerned: as a result they will have to be formally converted at or around the time of the mother's conversion, and they will carry the status of converts which means, in particular, that they cannot marry Cohanim. Waiting to get married until the gerus has been completed means that the children will be born as Jews of full status, able to marry anyone.

In the case of someone based in a country outside the United Kingdom, expert advice should be sought from someone who knows the religious communities of the country well to determine which Beth Din should be approached. In essence, though, the same advice applies as to the United Kingdom. Anyone coming up with clever solutions designed to save trouble and expense should be avoided like the plague: stick to the largest and most official organisation you can find. Even then, troubles can arise, as Rabbi Druckman's converts are now discovering (see Question 8): but at least the victims know that they made the most sensible choice possible, and that things would not have been easier for them if they had adopted one of the "quick and easy" options on offer.

Question 15 – Why should I have an orthodox conversion?

It is generally understood in the motoring world that even someone who fully intends to drive only automatic cars once he or she has passed the driving test is well advised to learn on a manual car. There are two reasons for this. First, automatic driving is easy: anyone who has mastered the intricacies of the rules and practices of using gears will be perfectly comfortable in an automatic car, but not the other way around. Secondly, the ease of automatic driving comes at a cost in various ways, and someone who has learned to drive a manual car may come when he or she looks again at automatics to appreciate the greater control and performance of a manual car – so they may alter their allegiance.

The analogy, although obvious, is flawed in several equally obvious ways.

First, someone who chooses to drive an automatic car is not effectively making the same choice for his or her children and grandchildren, condemning them to a limited range of cars. Secondly, a driving instructor will happily prepare a person for the driving test in a manual car despite their confessed intention to drive only automatics afterwards.

To convert to Judaism through a non-orthodox process is arguably pointless and certainly unwise. Unwise, because it prepares for your children and grandchildren a very significant risk of distress and confusion: unless you propose to inform them early and remind them continually that their status as Jews is not recognised by orthodox Judaism, they are likely to consider themselves "as Jewish as anyone else" and to mix freely and confidently in the wider Jewish world. They may never discover their (or your) mistake: but if they choose as a marriage partner someone from an orthodox background or if they simply become interested in practising Judaism according to orthodox rites, they will discover their mistake and it will certainly cause them trouble and may cause them unimaginable misery.

As I have made clear above, "regularisation" is not an easy option, and it will not always be an available option at all: the Beth Din will not be able to accept as a convert to orthodox Judaism someone who is committed to a non-orthodox community and who wishes to convert only in order to facilitate a marriage in an orthodox synagogue. Of course, the child or grandchild could always lie to the Beth Din about their motives and intentions: but deceit is not a good basis for any kind of religious practice (and I imagine is not sanctioned by non-orthodox leaders); nor, incidentally, would it make a promising foundation for a marriage.

So what would I advise someone to do if they want to convert through the Reform or another non-orthodox process, perhaps in order to facilitate a marriage, and they are absolutely certain that they have no commitment to orthodox Judaism?

My first reaction would be to invite them to satisfy themselves that they really do understand what orthodox Judaism is and why it is not for them. If anyone has kindly offered to explain to them what all the different kinds of Judaism involve, they should thank him or her kindly and ignore the offer. I would not consider myself qualified to explain to someone what progressive Judaism is about; and I am quite certain that anyone who does not practice orthodox Judaism cannot possibly understand it sufficiently, or be in sufficient sympathy with it, to explain it accurately to anyone else. So go to a progressive Jew to hear what he or she has to say about their religion: and then go to an orthodox Jew to hear what he or she (yes, the "or she" is intended and accurate) has to say about theirs.

If the result of that process is to affirm a person's commitment to non-orthodox Judaism, I would encourage them to think whether their conversion might be pointless: to put it another way, is your journey really necessary? As I understand it (and I know about non-orthodox Judaism only the little that has filtered through to me through the media from some of their higher-profile leaders) being non-Jewish is not a great disability within non-orthodox communities. "Mixed marriages" – which are simply not recognised as marriages within the orthodox community, are given a considerable degree of respect by the non-orthodox. I believe it is even possible to have a non-orthodox "Rabbi" attend a wedding ceremony between a Jew and a non-Jew and officiate in some capacity either at the ceremony itself or at some kind of blessing ceremony attached to it in some way. Certainly after the marriage, be it civil or religious or a mixture of the two, a non-Jewish partner will be welcomed within all or many non-orthodox communities, and will be subjected to little or nothing in the way of disability. At the same time it will be easy to explain to the children that one of their parents is not Jewish, which will put them on early and clear notice that their status is questionable according to orthodox tradition; or at least, if not easy, it will be easier than explaining that the conversion of one of their parents is valid only according to certain Jews. Each parent will have a clear and unequivocal religious status, and the children will know clearly from what position they start: and the journey to where the children may want to end up will be no more difficult.

Two important footnotes to this Question.

(1) The reader is referred to the Preface in which this book declares its intention to write from an unashamedly orthodox point of view, and not to attempt to give a balanced view.

(2) In describing certain things above I have referred to religious leaders of non-orthodox communities as "Rabbis" in inverted commas. I wish to state that I mean no personal disrespect by this. I am very well aware that leaders of the non-orthodox communities may be as deserving of respect and admiration as leaders of orthodox communities. I have heard much, for example, in praise of the late Hugo Grynn and the late Louis Jacobs from people whose opinions I value and respect: without doubt they were both enormously effective leaders and inspiringly sincere and spiritual believers. But for me the title Rabbi has a particular technical religious significance, signifying membership of a metaphorically unbroken chain of religious leadership beginning with Moses at Mount Sinai. As a matter of religious conviction I am required to reserve it as a term to describe leaders

who declare their intention to teach in accordance with the unbroken Sinaitic tradition, and anyone who declares their intention of instituting or countenancing deliberate departure from that tradition in any respect cannot be included within the term (Deuteronomy 13:3). Therefore as a matter of asserting my freedom of religious belief and expression, I feel obliged not to apply the term Rabbi to anyone who teaches any departure from orthodox Jewish practice as I understand it. This poses a dilemma: I do not wish to describe or address as Mr or Mrs anyone who describes themselves as Rabbi, but in the case of non-orthodox leaders my religious convictions prevent me from applying the term – so I have attempted a compromise by putting their title into inverted commas. I hope that, with the benefit of this explanation, they will acquit me of any discourteous or disrespectful intention and allow me the freedom to be as true to the tenets of my religious tradition as they are to theirs.

Question 16 – Is it really necessary to be so hard on prospective converts?

From first contact with a representative of the Jewish community to final interview with the Dayonim of a Beth Din, a prospective convert is likely to be exposed to delays, discouragement and behaviour which is the opposite of welcoming. Snubs rather than smiles may well be the enduring impression that they carry with them to success or, even worse, to eventual failure.

Although this attitude is not universal, it does have to be said that the more authentic the Judaism offered the more likely this attitude is likely to be prevalent, at least at an institutional level. There are, for example, internet websites that welcome prospective converts with electronically open arms and offer, either for an expressed fee or with a not-very hidden prospect of a donation in view, information, tuition and contacts galore. Service with a smile that is, however, unlikely to be a doorway to anything more than the remotest fringes of orthodoxy. The centre of orthodox observance and practice is guarded by local Rabbis and Botei Din whose general appearance to the new candidate is likely to be grim and forbidding at best; and rude and accusing at worst.

Of course, the orthodox world abounds with people whose love for their fellow human beings overflows and is constantly expressing itself in the form of cheerful smiles and welcoming homes. Hopefully, before too long the prospective convert will find one or more of them and build a constructive and friendly relationship with them. They will spend time with them in the local synagogue, and may well sit around their table on a Shabbos or Yom Tov – but however charming and genial they are, whenever the conversion process comes into the discussion their geniality is likely to freeze a little, and their normal frank expansiveness is likely to be exchanged for a slightly chilly prevarication. Understandably so, because they know that however inclined they might be to treat the candidate with friendly consideration, there is no point misleading him or her as to the nature of the treatment they are likely to encounter at the more official end of the exercise, particularly when dealing with the Beth Din.

So why is the official treatment of the Beth Din based upon prevarication, delay and what might generally be construed as a policy of obstruction? The underlying rationale is that because Judaism is not a proselytising religion and does not actively seek converts, we should actually incline a little towards the other extreme and be discouraging: in order to ensure that only those who are entirely genuine and sincere in their desire to become Jewish succeed in the attempt, the idea is to erect a not quite impenetrable barrier, the struggle through which will exclude those whose commitment is suspect.

But the notion that the most persistent candidate for conversion is also necessarily the most sincere, although widely held, seems to me misconceived. There are lots of reasons why a person may be put off by being rebuffed; and there are lots of reasons why a person may persist despite rebuffs. Not all of those reasons have anything to do with a person's belief in God or acceptance of the principles of the Jewish religion. Or, at least, not in the sense that the principle of active discouragement assumes: for instance, a person who has come to believe in one God and the principles of Jewish belief and practice of their own accord is more likely than not to have a very strong sense of humility and modesty – that may well cause him or her to react to a personal rebuff not by strengthening their resolve to renew the approach but by, in essence, taking themselves at the low value that they perceive other people to put on them. They may shrink away from exposing themselves to another snub not because of any lack of sincerity but because of their lack of self-confidence.

Workers in the field of "outreach" work within the Jewish community regularly remind each other how little space there may be between a person's first impulse to find out more about their religion and his or her turning their back on Judaism for ever. I knew one highly assimilated Jew who was walking past a Chassidish shul on Friday night when he suddenly had an urge to go inside and see what was going on. As he reached the doorway the sight of all the dark-clad figures in their outlandish round fur hats made him falter, and then, being a rather unusual person, he struck a deal with God: if the first person he went up to made him welcome, he would stay, and if not, he would leave and that would be the end of it. The first person he approached invited him for the Shabbos meal, he stayed for the whole of Shabbos; and now he is a Rabbi (as well as a university lecturer of unusual brilliance) living in a vibrant orthodox community. And it is not he who generally tells the story, but the man he first went up to in shul; he tells it as a warning to all orthodox Jews, even those of us who never had the intention of becoming "outreach" workers, that we may have that awesome responsibility suddenly thrust upon us.

In the case of converts there is a balance to be struck. On the one hand, if the Jewish community is too welcoming and friendly to people who express a vague and tentative interest in Judaism, we could be supplying social and other reasons for pursuing conversion, which would be contrary to the philosophy that only those with a sincere commitment to the principles of Judaism can become part of it. On the other hand, a genuine and sincere commitment to Judaism may perfectly easily be combined with a personality that is sensitive even to mild discourtesy; and by sending what appears to be a casual enquirer away with a flea in his or her ear one might be destroying the tender shoots of an important spiritual potential.

Most Botei Din who deal with gerus seems to get this balance right in some respects and wrong in others. So far as the Dayonim themselves are concerned, their ability to strike the right note on a personal level varies according to their natural capacities for communication: a small number are absolutely brilliant – I know of one in particular whose warmth and kindness are instantly apparent to anyone he meets, and whose sincerity and reliability are sufficiently obvious to make an impression even upon those whom he finds it necessary to delay or obstruct. Others clearly find it a little more difficult to combine making prospective candidates feel loved and cherished at a personal level with giving clarity about the necessary rigours of the conversion process and maintaining the distance appropriate to their position: not surprisingly, this being a combination that even highly trained educators or communicators find difficult. Taken as a whole, experiences with Dayonim at a personal level seem fairly positive, and are often exceedingly so. But the few half-hour sessions with the Dayonim that punctuate a person's journey towards conversion are only a tiny part of their experience of contact with the Beth Din; and the rest of the experience is not so good.

Generally speaking, the average experience is probably no worse than with any medium-size bureaucratic organisation: the occasional sullen and disinterested receptionist, failure to return calls, inflexible diaries, failure to stick to appointment times and so on. Nothing extreme, but overall an experience that is not significantly more pleasant or efficient than trying to change one's gas or electricity supplier. Which is disappointing and, in the circumstances, deplorable. Everything about the organisation and administration of a Beth Din should be redolent of the spiritual purpose for which it exists. In the same way that a Rabbi who is "one of the boys" is little or no use as a Rabbi – who must be someone who is not on my level but able to look down from his level and relate to me on mine – a Beth Din that fails to appear different from other bureaucracies is failing in its central purpose.

In particular, discouragement is one thing – and may or may not be necessary for a convert at different stages of the process – but rudeness is another. There is no excuse for any official of the Beth Din to exhibit bad manners towards anyone. And a receptionist, in particular, needs to be aware that he or she is not only the first point of encounter but may turn out to be the only one. A sullen and unhelpful receptionist could be enough single-handedly to deter a tentative but sincere inquiry from a prospective convert – and who knows what spiritual potential may not have been lost to the community and the world forever as the result of one piece of thoughtless rudeness, or a failure to take down a telephone message properly. I once saw a business whose telephone receptionists had a notice along the lines of "a lost call means lost business" above their heads: perhaps those at the Beth Din need a notice along the lines of "a lost call may mean a lost soul".

Question 17 – Why does Judaism not proselytise?

Children in Jewish primary schools or synagogue religion classes are habitually taught that one of the unique features of the Jewish religion is that it does not proselytise. Indeed we do not just teach our children this: it is sometimes made a central feature of "outreach" presentations to Jewish adults.

Like most things that are habitually taught as distinguishing Judaism from all other religions, it is wrong on one count and misleading on the other. As to the first, without professing to know anything significant about comparative religion it is easy to recognise that Judaism is not the only religion that does not actively seek to impose itself on others. While it is true that "spreading the word" is a fundamental part of many understandings of the Christian religion – although not all – there are other religions for whom converting others is not an aim, nor is it surprising that they should be the religions about which many of us know little or nothing.

But even as regards Judaism, the proposition that we do not proselytise is misleading. It is true that in the short-term there is no mission to convert members of other religious communities, or people without any religious commitment or tradition, to Judaism. More than that, we actively discourage converts, at least in the sense of setting the threshold of required commitment so high that it can be demonstrated only by someone prepared to persevere in the face of considerable, even if only passive, resistance and obstruction.

But the long-term Jewish aim is one of universal acceptance of the Jewish way of understanding the world. The liturgy abounds with scriptural references to the days in which the whole world will come to recognise a single God; although Rabbinic understandings of precisely what that means differ significantly, it is a common factor that the entire non-Jewish world will come to accept the authenticity of the Torah as expounded by the Rabbis. Where versions differ is in what the precise implications of that will be for the non-Jewish world; it may be that not all non-Jews will choose to become Jewish, but that they will simply co-exist in a state of co-operation. But it is clear that other religions will cease to operate, and that Judaism will be the single accepted universal truth.

Accusations of a Jewish desire for world domination are patently untrue in so far as they refer to a political or financial domination. The idea of a Jewish conspiracy to control the world is a recurring theme throughout the centuries – so that if there is a conspiracy it is clearly a singularly inefficient and unsuccessful one: but, unlike a number of other nations and even religions, there is no evidence that when the Jews have enjoyed national self-determination they have made any attempt to displace, or even influence, the cultures of even neighbouring areas. Indeed, the idea of two Jews agreeing about anything for long enough to attempt to form a conspiracy to dominate anyone else is sufficiently laughable to expose its own implausibility. Even in relation to the modern State of Israel one hears less the complaint that the Jews are trying to absorb and convert their neighbours and more the complaint that they are trying to marginalise and exclude non-Jews, including those who live within their undisputed borders: and even about the wisdom and propriety of that, there are as many different opinions as Jews, plus a few.

But in another sense, there is a sense in which Judaism must be said to have as a key component of its long-term agenda not the domination of the world by Jews but the acceptance by the world of Judaism. That may or may not imply an eventual mass conversion to Judaism, depending on how one chooses to understand different Rabbinic pictures of the Messianic age: but it certainly requires that the whole world – starting with the Jews and spreading from them – comes to accept the purity and divinity of the Torah way of life, as it applies to all aspects of human behaviour, from business ethics to animal welfare. (If it occurs to the reader that it is arguable that in relation to those two particular examples there are no large contemporary Jewish communities that are particularly conspicuous for upholding Torah values, that only goes to demonstrate the fact that is well-known to most religious Jews, that of all communities in the world today the one most urgently in need of becoming Jewish is our own.)

If universal acceptance of Judaism is an eventual goal, according to one understanding or another of what it will mean in practice, why do we not start now in a small way, by encouraging converts where we can?

There are two reasons for this, closely connected.

The first is simply that the picture painted by the Torah is consistently one of people flocking to gather in and around the Jewish community of their own accord, attracted by a shining example of spiritually and ethically satisfying behaviour; nowhere in Jewish sources does one find encouragement, or even permission, to force anyone to become Jewish, or to exert military or any other kind of pressure to that end. Classical Judaism is neither pacifist nor tolerant of other religions, in the sense of being prepared to admit that we do not have a monopoly of truth: but despite that there is no concept of compulsion to become Jewish, although there is a concept of compulsion to abandon the worship of idols, while choosing to live within a Jewish State.

The second reason why we do not encourage conversion now, which flows from the first, is that until we are providing to the world a working model of Judaism in practice it all its ramifications, there is nothing to invite people to join. What we have at present, in the state of exile that exists even within the borders of the modern State of Israel and for as long as the Sanhedrin and Temple have not been re-established, is merely a personal Judaism, a stop-gap mixture of remembrances of the past and foretastes of the future, capable of helping individuals to achieve personal spiritual fulfilment but incapable of demonstrating how the wider systems of the Torah are intended to work. Anybody who joins us now is buying into a pale imitation of the real thing, a temporary arrangement of which the best that can be said is that it contains the seeds that are capable of blossoming at any moment into something powerful and permanent.

So while we have no right to deny someone who is determined to join us in our prolonged flight through exile to redemption, they join at their own urging, and despite their understanding that we have at this present juncture in our history very little of worth to offer them as a nation. Our discouragement is necessary to ensure that they fully understand what they are getting – or more importantly what they are not getting; and it would be dishonest in the extreme openly to encourage people from communities outside us to join what we know to be a fundamentally flawed community. Once we have succeeded in turning ourselves as a community into something approaching what we ought to be, then the issue of encouragement will fall away; people will indeed come to join us, and will be most welcome, once they can see the hand of God in the way the Jewish world works – and until that time there is nothing worth joining.

Question 18 – What status do converts have in the Jewish community?

In two words: undeservedly low.

For all the reasons discussed in Question 4, converts ought to be regarded with a mixture of awe and admiration. There should be intense competition to attract them to marry into ones family, and they should generally be made to feel loved, wanted and respected.

It is indeed a positive commandment of the Torah to love those who convert, and the Torah even goes so far as to remind us to have affection and compassion for them because their initial experience as strangers in our community should remind us of the unpleasant experience of being strangers in other "host" communities in our times, starting with Egypt.

Even if there were no commandment to love the ger, one would expect his or her journey and devotion to command a respect and inspire an affection in all who see it merely as a matter of human instinct (which is of course a reflection of the instinct of the Divinity in whose image we are made). Probably, God only included an express commandment to love the ger because He was able to make a depressingly accurate guess as to how we would otherwise be inclined to treat them. Even with the express commandment, the reality is pretty grim, and fully supports the notion discussed in Question 4 that we see converts as a shameful reflection on our own comparative lack of devotion and religious commitment.

I have been told by numerous people, in numerous and very different parts of the Jewish community, that one or other person is a convert. The tone of voice in which the announcement is made has varied, but only within a certain limited range: I have been told it with an inflection which implies compassionate understanding - "one shouldn't expect too much of so and so because his or her father or mother is a ger"; I have been told it in a tone which implies explanation that he or she is bound to be a bit strange - "well she is a giyoret, you know"; I have even been told it in a tone of voice which implies an excuse for why the speaker is reluctantly being nice to the person - "Actually, I wanted to include him because he's a convert: but he's actually a really interesting person …"; and I have heard it used to add to the worth of someone being praised, as though he or she deserves extra credit for being a decent or impressive human being having had such an unhappy start - "and did you know that he's actually a ger?". Significantly, I have never had anyone say to me in a voice of hushed admiration, such as they would use in pointing out the close descendant of a prominent Rabbi, "do you see that woman - she is a giyoret!" I have also never actually had anyone say to me in a protesting tone of voice "some of my best friends are gerim", because the protestation would almost certainly be too absurd to attract credence: but, as with certain other minority groups, the general idea that converts are a class against whom there is prejudice which threatens to taint us all and causes us occasionally to protest our own freedom from its infection is prevalent.

In particular, the idea that there should be competition to attract gerim to marry into ones family is very much the converse of what happens in practice. I stood once in a group of orthodox Jews standing around at a buffet breakfast while our children fought in the corner. For some reason that I have forgotten a mention was made of converts as a class, in a manner or tone that was clearly slighting. I demurred gently, and caused a particularly distinguished member of the group, a respected member of a prominent orthodox synagogue in Golders Green, to turn to me with a slight sneer and remark something along the lines of "That's all very well but you wouldn't want your daughter to marry one, would you?", a remark that was received by the group generally as a particularly apposite put-down. "Well," I replied hesitantly," as it happens I wouldn't mind at all, because, you see ...," the group hushed and leaned forward slightly, delighted to have elicited what appeared about to be a confidence about the Greenberg genealogy as a result of which they would be able to show a condescending and superior affability, "you see," I added in a brisker tone, "I happen not to be an ignorant bigot - but," I added reassuringly, "I can see that I were an ignorant bigot I might mind dreadfully." The group dispersed.

Bigotry it undoubtedly is, but prevalent it also certainly is, particularly in the more conservative, "black hat" circles. Anyone approaching a shadchan – a professional arranger of marriages within the orthodox Jewish community – and identifying themselves or their parents as a convert, will not be greeted by rapturous assurances of the certainty of an excellent match. They will be greeted by anything from complete discouragement to a sympathetic assurance that the shadchan will do their best: thereafter they are likely to find themselves sent to meet girls or boys who, to put it bluntly, all have some obvious problem or deficiency and are being matched with a ger on the implicit understanding that conversion too is a black mark in the shiduch market.

I heard from a prominent and enormously respected Rabbi in Israel with whom I discussed the issue of gerus that he advises gerim who are setting out on a shiduch meeting that they are not obliged to mention their status as gerim until the third or fourth meeting. The clear implication was that this is some kind of defect that may discourage a possible partner, and that they will therefore wish to hide it for as long as possible; it therefore becoming necessary to determine as a matter of halachah for how long a person is permitted not to disclose it. This particular Rabbi clearly felt he was going out on a limb to be helpful to gerim by allowing them to suppress their status for as much as three or four meetings, by which time their good qualities will hopefully have asserted themselves and formed an attraction for the sake of which the other party would be prepared to overlook the ger's status. He implied that in taking this strong line he had encountered a certain amount of opposition, and asked whether I agreed with his approach: my reply was that I strongly disagreed with the idea that a ger's status is anything to be ashamed of in any way at all, and that on the contrary it should in very many cases be seen as a "selling point" in a shiduch, so that there should be no need to suppress the status even at a first meeting. He agreed with this very strongly, but on the grounds that it was the ideal position: the reality, however, he said is simply not like that, and as a Rabbi giving practical advice to individuals one has to be realistic ...

In the next edition of this book I hope to able to report that this Question was read by a number of converts who have contacted me to assure me that my description does not at all reflect their own experience, and that they have been welcomed with open arms from all corners of the orthodox Jewish world and have never been made to feel belittled or slighted in any way. But I am not holding my breath. If I receive any reaction to this Question from gerim I expect it to be sadly confirmatory.

However, the real purpose of this Question is to hope (also probably forlornly) that it will be read by members of the orthodox establishment and that it may encourage them to think again about whether as a community we are doing enough to comply with the commandment to love the ger. It is not enough to have vaguely or even positively benign feelings towards them, however genuine: the commandment to love is a commandment to put that love into action, and to think about ways of ensuring that the common experience of the ger is not that of the uncomfortable outsider: we are reminded by the Torah of our experience in Egypt and elsewhere in the hope that it will encourage us to structure our community in a way that mitigates any disadvantage that may affect gerim.

For example, it is often noted with pride by Jews and admiration by non-Jews that the Jewish community sets a wonderful example of emphasis on family life. Non-Jews tasked with making patronising speeches about the Jewish community find this a safe favourite line, "how much we have learned from Jewish family values". But there are two ways of telling that story. If Judaism is seen at its best in the close nuclear family clustered around the Shabbos table, how much more difficult it must be for people who, for whatever reason, do not have their own close-knit family circle, to feel a full part of the community. Clearly, this is an issue that affects many people other than gerim; but it is likely to affect gerim in particular. Particularly before marriage, they are more likely than other people to lack the supportive network of siblings and parents, and they will certainly lack the surrogate participation in the community that many of us derive from our families. Unmarried converted young women will probably participate in the synagogue services as little as other unmarried women; but they will not receive the news from, and be regarded as an included appurtenance of, their father who attends the synagogue twice a day. After marriage, they will hopefully have the support of their spouse, but when young children come along they are likely not to receive the same kind of day-to-day practical support that many young Jewish couples receive from the grand-parents.

What are we doing as a community to address this? Nothing. What could we do? Lots.

In particular, the Beth Din that handles every gerus should also assign to the ger one or more families as adoptive families to be responsible for their transition into the community. This might be the family with whom the ger lived and learned while going through the process: but there is no reason why it need be. The family should be required to report regularly to the Beth Din, so that for at least the first five years of a ger's membership of the community the Dayonim are taking, and are seen to be taking, an active part in the ger's life. The Dayonim should encourage "their" gerim to use them as sponsors and referees in the matter of shiduchim, and should generally satisfy themselves that everything is well, not just by casual inquiries or passive availability, but by actively pursuing every possible avenue of easing the ger's early Jewish life.

Every community should also take responsibility for ensuring that it runs itself in a way that makes as many events and facilities as accessible as possible for gerim and others who lack a close family circle. Arranging for invitations to families is common and praiseworthy; but it is not enough, because it maintains a position of inequality. The ger or other person invited to a family feels constantly that they are being done a favour to, by being included in the "ideal" of a family unit so that they are not alone for Shabbos or Yom Tov. Communities need to structure themselves more so that gerim, single people or other people who may feel at some kind of a social disadvantage are able to feel more on terms of equality with the rest of the community. Not the occasional "singles lunch" hosted by the Rabbi (which can be reminiscent of the meal given by Edward Dorrit to the residents of the Marshalsea on his departure – "an ounce of plum pudding and a ton of patronage"): but regular meals and other events for the whole community, which it becomes the norm for as many members of the community as possible, including those with large and exciting families, to attend as a matter of course.

In the meantime, what can one advise the ger about how to make the best of his or her social status?

First, make a careful choice of the community within which you intend to live, and, in particular, the shuls where you intend to pray. Either of two extremes will be fine.

Either choose an enlightened modern orthodox environment, a community whose members are serious about their Judaism and equally serious about making a positive contribution to, and deriving selective benefit from, the modern world. In that community you should find yourself valued for what you are, and not pre-judged unfavourably by reference to ignorant misconceptions about who you are, where you have come from and how and why you came from it.

If that kind of Judaism does not appeal to you, go to the other extreme – choose a vibrant Chareidi community and be honest with it early on about who and what you are. Your status will be treated as a disability – which is a monstrous way of seeing it – but once you have decided to accept that hurdle you should find that you are accepted with a genuinely benign desire to accommodate you and your disability. You will be a second-class citizen, and your children will have to fight harder than other people's to achieve recognition and status, simply because they do not come from an illustrious lineage. Some might think (as I do) that this is appalling and to be avoided at all costs – but you may feel differently. You may be attracted to the Chareidi world and be satisfied to join it on its own terms. Fair enough: no accounting for tastes.

What I would most strenuously advise against, however, is joining a community that is neither one thing nor the other: a community that has neither the breadth of mind of the genuinely modern genuinely orthodox nor the strict decency and values of the genuinely meticulous Chareidim. In certain communities their lack of real spiritual credentials is compensated for by strict adherence to the inessentials, and in particular the empty bigotries that lead to looking down upon anyone from the outside. In such a community you are likely to be treated as second-class, not openly but behind your back, and without any of the compensating attempts to assist and absorb you.

When it comes to shiduchim, take as active a part in the process yourself as you can. Do not simply put yourself in the hands of one or more of the professional shadchanim (match-makers) and expect to be fairly and sensibly treated. By all means contact professional shadchanim as well as pursuing other avenues: but discuss with the shadchan how she intends to treat your status as a ger. If the answer is that she thinks it irrelevant, do not use her – there is nothing irrelevant about your gerus: it speaks volumes about who you are and what qualities you have, and should be seen as a valuable asset that requires matching by equal strength of character in anyone proposed as a potential partner. If the answer is that your status as a ger is regrettable, but that the shadchan will do her best for you, put the 'phone down.

There is a strong concept in Jewish theory that yichus – lineage – is important when it come to making a marriage choice. In a number of places the Rabbis advise us to examine the family of anyone we propose to marry before making a decision. But the examination has to be made not merely from a superficial perspective: in particular, it does not mean that you have to like and admire everyone in your partner's family, and it certainly does not mean that you have to share all their values or beliefs. It means principally two things.

First, that you must examine your partner's character in the light of their family and other associations, both to understand their character better and to see something of the people after whom they are likely to take in some way or another: so you need to approve their family as human beings, possessed of sense and decency.

Secondly, that you must be satisfied that the culture into which you are marrying is a congenial one: but when a person marries a ger he or she is not marrying into their former family's religious culture, from which they have chosen to separate themselves, so this aspect of the Rabbis' advice becomes irrelevant at least to some extent.

The most difficult thing for a giyoret to understand is that she is not permitted to marry a Cohen. I once heard the question why this should be the case posed in a youth group "Ask the Rabbi" panel session, by a boy who had been converted, alongside his sister, at an early age at the time when his mother converted. The resentment and indignation in his voice was apparent to us all, and was probably all the stronger given that it was, in effect, felt vicariously on his sister's behalf. The first answer offered came from a Rabbi who had married into a family of Cohanim: he wittered on about how holy his wife's family were and how he only fully came to realise it when he watched her cleaning the windows – or some such nonsense. Not merely ducking the question, but exacerbating its force. Another couple of relatively anodyne answers were offered along the same kind of lines but sufficiently muddled to be less inflammatory. My offering was simply to agree that it does seem enormously unfair and that I have never understood it. Having puzzled about it on and off over the years, I still think it seems unfair and I still do not understand it. I am absolutely clear that the Torah was never intended to operate in a way that implies that a ger is spiritually inferior: the full expression Ger Tzedek – which can be roughly translated as a righteous stranger – would be sufficient to counter that thought.

So then I am left with a simple Biblical prohibition that I cannot understand – but then the Torah is replete with prohibitions that I cannot understand. Perhaps it has something to do with the fact that at times when the Temple service is in operation the Cohanim are intended and expected to develop such an intense and particular culture that nobody who comes from completely outside the system could reasonably be expected to adapt to it upon marriage. But perhaps not.

To conclude on this Question, much depends on the personality and wishes of each ger. Some wish only to blend into a particular community, and have their origins forgotten as quickly as possible by them and others around them: that is their right, and should be respected. But that is not necessarily the most healthy attitude, and it should certainly not be seen as the ideal. A ger should not have to eclipse part of who he or she is, and his or her family history, in order to be an accepted and important part of our community. You acquire an adoptive family, but that does not mean you stop being proud of your natural family (and as to keeping in contact with them see Question 21).

I have attended various family celebrations of a family whose mother is a particularly impressive convert; the speeches regularly focus on a particular experience in their recent family history which for good cultural reasons is not shared by any of their friends but which is capable of teaching them a great deal, and is certainly something to be proud of. It ought to stand to reason that a ger should be able to stand up in public and celebrate his or her family history, rather than constantly suppressing it for fear that it should prejudice the next generation's marriage prospects.

Question 19 – So what does the convert get out of the process?

On the surface, a person gets little or nothing out of becoming Jewish. The most obvious reward of becoming Jewish is that the convert gets to share in any persecution or obloquy that is the lot of the Jews from time to time. But despite the obviously tempting nature of this benefit, it does seem a little hard that while sharing any hardships that happen to be going in any particular generation the ger cannot even feel the satisfaction of having acquired a status of equality.

Socially speaking, converts are regarded by most Jewish people as inherently inferior to those of Jewish descent. This is as remorselessly true as it is senseless and indefensible. While we should be proud of and inspired by those who come sometimes from very far away to join us, they perhaps remind us too starkly of our own failure to live up to the spiritual heritage to which they have aspired and which they generally guard and appreciate better than those who inherited it. For whatever reason, a convert is nowhere regarded as the pinnacle of achievement and respectability, and in almost all seriously orthodox circles is universally patronised and belittled.

Generally speaking, the only thing converts can be sure of is that while they will not count as really Jewish to Jews, they will count as really Jewish, or even worse than really Jewish, when it comes to attracting the hostility and antagonism of antisemites or more generally ill-disposed persons. The lout who shouts obscenities from a passing car at a group of people emerging from the synagogue on a Sabbath morning tends not to include an express exemption from his remarks for any converts who may happen to be among them: nor is the stone hurled from across the road any more discriminating. A convert anywhere outside Israel can be fairly confident that by adopting the outward appearances of Jewish observance he or she will acquire no material advantage, but a good deal of material troubles of many different kinds, which will do their best to compensate for any spiritual advantage that may accrue as a result of the change of status. This has remained so constantly true over the course of the ages that the Talmud remarks that during any of the many times of persecution for the Jewish people one may accept a prospective convert immediately, without any examination of his or her motives or aspirations, on the grounds that nothing but sincere belief in the truth of the Jewish religion could lead anyone to be so insane as to wish to share our fate.

So why bother? If the convert's lot is so one-sidedly not a happy one, what possible reason could there be for pursuing conversion?

The real and rather sad explanation in many cases is that potential converts have an impressively thorough theoretical knowledge of Judaism and blessedly little knowledge of or prior exposure to Jews. In every generation it has been Jews who are most likely to put other people off Judaism. If one knows about Judaism only what one has read in books, one could be excused for finding it rather attractive. And it must be difficult for converts who have not mixed much or at all in the orthodox community to imagine just how inhumanly some people will be capable of behaving to them once they have converted.

Compelling though this explanation is, however, it is deficient in one respect. A person who has a really thorough knowledge of Jewish theology will know that he or she is actually just as well off spiritually out as in, even from the perspective of that theology. Or, indeed, a great deal better off. One of the few points upon which Jewish abstract theology is relatively clear is that a meritorious non-Jew is as certain of being allowed into the world to come as is a meritorious Jew. The big difference, however, is that while the Jew will be judged by the Almighty against the standard of meticulous observance of all 613 Biblical commandments (including those pertaining to business and social ethics) the non-Jew will be judged by reference only to compliance with the seven Noachide laws.

On one occasion a boy who had been studying in an ultra-orthodox yeshivah for some years received some distressing intelligence. His parents had done some genealogical research in the course of which it had become apparent that they were halachically not Jewish. The whole family was arranging for a formal conversion through the Beth Din which had, of course, undertaken to make the process expeditious in the unusual circumstances. The boy asked to take a few days to think over the news. Having done so, he told the head of the academy that in accordance with his understanding of Jewish theology he was far better off spiritually remaining non-Jewish: he thought he could manage a reasonably conscientious observance of the seven Noachide laws – particularly since he felt no particular desire to eat a limb torn off a living animal – but he was much less complacent about the remaining 606. So, on the whole, he thought he would decline to convert. Off he went, and that was the last the Jewish community ever saw of him. His reaction was socially and communally puzzling and disturbing, but theologically sound.

So a perfect abstract knowledge of Jewish theology is more likely to keep a person away from conversion than to persuade him or her into it, so we may need to look beyond abstract theology to discover what it is that inspires people to join us. It may be that these few prospective converts who are fired with genuine spiritual enthusiasm have met one or other of those few hidden Jews whose behaviour and thought are an unlimited inspiration to spiritual achievement. The Rabbis teach of thirty-six completely righteous people who live in each generation, and without whose purity the world would not be deemed worthy to survive. By their nature they are most unlikely to be acclaimed religious leaders, because it is almost (although not quite) impossible to be praised and courted on all sides on account of one's spiritual purity without losing it, if it ever existed, in the process. They are more likely to be the genuinely unassuming who are sincerely unaware of their own particular merits, since it never occurs to them to judge themselves favourably by comparison with the standards of those around them; on the contrary, to the extent that they permit themselves to form a judgment about other people's behaviour, they put so favourable a construction upon it, in accordance with the old Rabbinic requirement, as to emerge from the comparison feeling in need of renewed efforts in the way of self-improvement.

It may be that we all meet at least one of these people, because God likes to give every one of us a chance to recognise sincerity and be inspired by it: but in general, the opportunity passes by without recognition. Perhaps some of the prospective converts who actually believe in Judaism, do so because they have met one of the very few people who actually practices it.

Alternatively, some gerim may have entered the community without any illusion about the spiritual nature and quality of the majority of their adoptive brethren. Their motivation may be simply that they have set for themselves exacting standards of spiritual attainment, that require more than compliance with the seven Noachide laws can deliver. Someone whose soul thirsts to come as close as possible to the Divine, will not be content with anything less than acceptance of the burden of the Divine command, as formulated in the 613 commandments discovered by Abraham and then transmitted by God to Moses.

Whatever factor inspires each of the small number of "real" converts each year to become Jewish, the sincerity of their spiritual ambition provides a vital inspiration for the rest of us, Jews and non-Jews alike. As has been mentioned above Rabbinic literature compares converts to a disfiguring disease that afflicts the Jewish nation. This apparently gratuitous piece of harshness attracts a number of different explanations, as one would expect. The most trite is that it refers only to those converts who are not genuine, but convert in order to attain some collateral advantage, perhaps in business or matrimonial prospects. The most satisfying is that the intention of the statement is that the presence in our midst of a group of people who had every reason to ignore the Torah instead of which they have whole-heartedly embraced it and devotedly uphold and implement its values, is a constant reproach to those of us who have allowed familiarity to breed contempt, and as continual a provocation as galling as any sore. This graphic metaphor could explain much about the habitual contempt for the *ger tzedek* – the righteous convert: their presence offends us because it reminds us of how deplorably casually we treat our own birthright. We look down on them for fear that if we do not we might come to look down on ourselves, and weep tears of shame and despair.

Question 20 – What kind of Jew should I become?

Early in the process of becoming acquainted with the Jewish community the prospective ger will realise that Jews come in many different cultural shapes and sizes. Looking at all the different traditions of dress, liturgy and other ritual matters, the ger may feel that he or she is spoiled for choice. Unlike Jews who take their tradition from their family, unless they find a very strong reason to change at some point in their life, the ger has the luxury of choice, which brings with it the difficulty of knowing what to choose: so how should you choose to which kind of community within the orthodox tradition to belong?

The most important message is that to begin with you should put the question out of your mind, and concentrate on acquiring the basic common denominators of the religion. Contrary to what one might think from the fuss that is made about them, the cultural differences that divide the different orthodox communities are mostly irrelevant to the religious essentials. Their members are principally distinguished in the matter of dress, for example, and yet as a matter of religious theory provided that a man covers his head, at least at times of saying prayers, learning Torah or involvement in other religious matters, and provided his head covering is large enough to cover the majority of his head, it is of absolutely no importance whatsoever whether he is wearing a brown fur hat of a fashion originated by the Russian Cossacks, a black felt trilby in the modern Italian style, or a multi-coloured knitted tea-cosy contraption manufactured by his sister. The essentials of Judaism, blessings before and after eating, the morning, afternoon and evening prayers, the key observances of Shabbos and Yom Tov, are indistinguishable at a level of basic Biblical law and only begin to diverge in relatively recent and peripheral matters of Rabbinic development and community custom.

So the prospective ger should obtain a solid grounding in the basics first, and these will stand him or her in good stead irrespective of to which part of the community they are eventually attracted. A good tutor of a gerus candidate will teach very much along "neutral" lines, without reference to the flavour of the community to which he or she belongs. There is plenty of time after the conversion process has been completed for the ger to start to move towards any particular extreme or less extreme version of Jewish culture that appear attractive: until that point the priority is to concentrate on the essentials.

Having said that, a good tutor will find time to explore some of the cultural variations and different traditions on different matters, but being careful always to start by teaching, and distinguishing, the basic and "neutral" basic rules. And if the prospective ger has already had an opportunity to develop an interest in a particular style or community (perhaps, in the case of a marriage or regularisation case, as a result of family involvement) there should be plenty of opportunity to expand a little on the relevant customs and traditions, without detracting from the key task of absorbing the essentials.

Question 21 – Need conversion cut me off from my family and friends?

As a matter of Jewish law, upon conversion a person acquires an entirely new identity, as a result of which he or she ceases technically to be related to their former family. A convert is given a Hebrew name, for which purpose they can choose any first name they like, and in place of the normal patronymic by reference to their natural father they are referred to as "son of Abraham our Father" or "daughter of Sarah our Mother".

This can cause particular difficulty, and embarrassment, in a "regularisation" case involving a Jewish father and a mother who either is not Jewish according to any standard or is the product of a non-orthodox conversion. Although the father may be entirely ignorant of all matters of Jewish law and ritual, that is far from necessarily the case: it often happens that those who have deliberately rejected some or all of the Jewish tradition have done so from a base of more knowledge and understanding than is possessed by many of those who remain loyal to the orthodox tradition. The result is that the father may be alert to the fact that until now his son has been called up to the reading of the Torah as So and So the son of (the father's own name); hearing him suddenly called up as the son of

Abraham our Father is a metaphorical slap in the face, that could be harder to bear than any of the confusion and disruption that the family may have suffered so far in the conversion process. There is some possible support for the notion that in a case of this kind it might be permitted to continue calling a son up by reference to his father's name, but it is unlikely to find favour in most orthodox circles. There is no need, however, to be insensitive as well as intransigent, and a convert should be meticulous to ask the officials of his synagogue, on any occasion when his father may happen to be present, either not to call him up at all or, if it is unavoidable (as it would be, for example, if the reason why his father is present is to celebrate his son's approaching marriage, having been made possible by the conversion process) then to ensure that the names are pronounced in an indistinct way. Given the tumult normally prevailing during intervals in the reading of the Torah while people are being called up, this should not be too challenging a demand, and the officials must certainly comply with it, remembering that the prohibition against embarrassing a fellow human-being is as powerful and urgent as any other Torah prohibition.

Of course, where the father was a Cohen, there will be no disguising the fact that the son is not a Cohen, and he will be called up to the Torah not for the first section, as is the right of Cohanim, but as one of the remaining five after Cohen and Levy. No sensitivity on the part of the officials of the synagogue can disguise the fact that the father cut his children off (doubtless unwittingly, owing to faulty education or understanding) from their rightful inheritances both as Jews and as members of a distinguished lineage within Judaism – and that only one of those is remediable by the joint efforts of the son himself and the Rabbis who facilitate his conversion, thereby restoring him to at least part of what his father denied him.

Leaving aside the question of when the father happens to be present, issues arise in relation to the correct procedure in calling a convert to the Torah. In some cases, to put it bluntly, a person is embarrassed to be identified publicly as a convert, which will certainly happen if he is called up to the Torah as "the son of Abraham our Father".

Once again, sense and sensitivity are called for.

In a "regularisation" case, it does not matter how impressively and inspiringly a person has behaved in undergoing the rigours of the conversion process in order to restore themselves to a status they had always assumed that they had; it is inevitable that in the presence of their friends with whom they may have grown up, they will be reluctant to keep harking back to the fact that for all those years they were, in one sense, living a lie. And even in the absence of their parents they may dislike the imputation against their family's behaviour that may be read into the public reiteration of their converted status. In such a case there is solid halachic support for suppressing the "Our Father" and simply calling the person up as "son of Abraham", in which case he is indistinguishable from any other person whose father happens to be called Abraham.

There are, however, very strong reasons for not suggesting or encouraging this in any case other than one of regularisation where the potential embarrassment is particularly significant. For the general case, a convert should both be treated with respect and admiration by the community and should also feel proud of his or her achievement in joining our community. Nothing done in relation to calling people up to the reading of the Torah should give any convert reason to suspect either that he should be ashamed of his own status, or that any of the officials or congregants might think that there is anything to be ashamed of in being a convert. The title "Son of Abraham Our Father" should be a badge that a convert can wear in public with a proper modicum of pride.

All this might be called the technical aspect of the convert's relationship with his previous family. The emotional and practical issues are less clear-cut, but enormously important. There is nothing tolerant about Judaism, when it comes to how we see other religions. There is nothing bigoted about Judaism, when it comes to how we see human beings. When a convert who previously belonged to a family of adherents to any religion, his or her choice to leave that religion and become Jewish cannot be interpreted in any light other than as a spirited rejection of that religion in favour of the tenets of the Torah. There is no room in Judaism for a pluralist "In my father's palace there are many rooms" approach: the liturgy is steeped with references to the exclusiveness of God and of the truth of our perception of Him. The convert cannot look back at his family's religious observances and say to them "You have chosen the truth, but I have chosen a different truth".

All of which might seem to be an unpromising start to the prospect of a convert's enjoying a productive relationship with his or her family after conversion. The reality, however, is the opposite. As in all questions of inter-faith relations, the greatest bar to progress is equivocation. If two people look at each other and each says "I reject the truth of your religion but I value you as a human being and would like to deal with you on equal terms based on shared humanity", there is complete honesty at the start which provides an excellent basis for co-operation in most if not all human endeavours. But if we start by trying to hide from each other the extent to which our religions oppose each other at a theoretical level, focusing on if not actually exaggerating areas in respect of which the message happens to be either genuinely the same or superficially similar, and hoping that we will never scratch sufficiently deeply below the surface of our religions to expose their real incompatibilities, our relationship is based on a deliberate dishonesty and evasion which cannot deliver a lasting friendship at a human level.

The same goes for the particular instance of the convert approaching his or her family, whether they belong to a different religion or to none. The most promising start that can be made is along the following lines, tempered and presented in a way that most suits the particular personalities and circumstances.

> "Dear Mum and Dad,
>
> I have decided to become Jewish.
>
> This is going to cause some tension between us. In particular, it means that I have thought about the way you brought me up, and I have chosen to depart from it to some extent. I expect you to feel

extremely unhappy about this, because your values and beliefs are as important to you as my new values and beliefs are to me.

But I would like us to focus on the positive. I want you to know how many of the values that you taught me are not just compatible with my new religion, but are essential parts of it.

For example, Judaism requires me to be honest, taking the concept in its widest application to all aspects of life. That is a rather tall order: but I start off at a considerable advantage, having been able to learn from your example of honesty and decency in conducting relationships with other people. On a level of personal qualities and humanity there is so much you taught me by example and that I am taking with me as a vital foundation for my new religious life, so that from my side what I am doing now does not feel like a rejection of you or your values at a personal level.

There will be a few practical difficulties to sort out. I hope we will always feel not just welcome in, but actually part of, each other's homes: but obviously I will now only be eating kosher food, so I will need to ask for your tolerance in humouring my new rules of food ingredients and preparation. I dare say this is not the first time I have made unreasonable demands on you, but hopefully we can actually find some practical solutions that make this new request not too difficult to satisfy!

Your ever-loving son / daughter,"

In reality, kashrus and other ritual laws should not present too great a practical barrier to continuing a mutually satisfying relationship with a convert's former family. To some extent, however, this depends on where and how the family live. In London, for example, such a wide variety of kosher food is so easily available that parents who want to prepare food for visiting children and grandchildren can do so easily enough. But practicalities quickly become entangled with emotional issues: cooking for ones children and serving them at ones table own can for some parents be a very significant part of the family experience. Being told that your child can no longer eat the food that comes out of your pots and pans can be devastating: nor should those who take these things lightly (or who flatter themselves that they would take them lightly were they on the receiving end) underestimate their emotional significance for others. And so much depends on circumstances: a family who pride themselves on keeping an elegant table, well-presented with fine crockery and cutlery, will be significantly disrupted by being asked to serve their child from now on when he or she visits only using disposables; while for other families this will not be a problem at all.

The first key to making all this work is thinking in advance, what might cause offence or distress, and how it can best be avoided or minimised. No one solution will fit all personalities and circumstances, but in almost all cases a little open and honest communication at the right time – generally earlier rather than later – will enable the right solution to be found.

The second key is flexibility. A convert may have decided to impose on himself or herself the most stringent of standards in relation to a particular law of kashrus. Fine and laudable. But when contemplating a visit home to his or her parents, the question becomes whether rigidity in those standards is worth the potential cost in terms of diminishing closeness to their parents. In this area as in all others, the convert needs a Rabbi who is an expert in all four sections of the Shulchan Aruch code, plus the fifth – commonsense. To say "forbidden" is easy: to find a creative solution to a problem within the parameters of the Shulchan Aruch requires greater halachic expertise and an active and intelligent mind. Many converts will be surprised at how much room there is for movement within the parameters of halachah to make it easier to observe the rules of kashrus while eating in their parents' home: but for this to work, all possible practical difficulties need to have been thought of in advance and anticipated by the adoption of one halachic solution or another. An hour's tea-party in the convert's former family home could take three hour's preparation in conference with a Rabbi: the ideal result is that the family remain unaware that any special preparations or solutions have had to be made or found at all.

Of course, not all converts will have had a particularly close relationship with their family to begin with: but for those who did, and who want to maintain it, the message is that with thought and care it should be possible. As with most things in life, if one sets out to look for problems one will find only problems, but if one sets out to look for solutions as well one will, at least much of the time, find them.

There are a number of other technical and practical aspects of relations with the convert's former family. This is not the place to discuss them in any detail, partly because this book is not intended as an exhaustive and authoritative halachic treatise, and partly because the permutations and combinations of circumstance would make it impossible to provide useful guidance without writing at enormous length.

But the convert should not assume that anything is impossible or that any obstacle is insuperable: nor indeed, that problems can be ignored until they arise. Timely discussion from all possible angles with a sensible and knowledgeable Rabbi is the only wise approach.

So far as the convert's friends before conversion are concerned, the picture is to some extent similar to that for his or her family. With creative thinking, much is possible. But one also needs to be realistic. It may be that the convert has been socialising almost exclusively in Jewish circles for some time, but maybe not – and there is certainly no reason why that should be the case. Whatever the case, it is salutary for the convert to remind himself or herself before completing the conversion process that whatever good intentions are formed on all sides about keeping up with former friends, the reality may turn out to fall short of those intentions for unavoidable reasons, some purely practical and some less so.

As to practical reasons, parents can be expected to put up with a good deal of trouble from their children in order to preserve the possibility of a good continuing relationship. A mother and father will happily watch boiling water poured over their kitchen counters – and probably do the pouring themselves – if that is the price of being able to entertain their grandchildren to tea.

Friends can be expected to be less accommodating. What one can ask of a friend is less than one can ask of a parent. And yet the same tensions exist, and once one can no longer eat and drink in a friend's house, a barrier is created which prevents the continuation of uninhibited discourse.

More than that, however, developing lifestyles create their own tensions and incompatibilities which arise in all kinds of circumstances, not just in the context of conversion, and have to be accepted with good grace as part of life. A convert who used to meet a group of friends every month or so for a drink or two in the pub, might start out with the intention of maintaining the tradition: he or she might remind themselves that the technical halachic difficulties of joining friends for a drink in a pub are trivial and all resolvable. But after a while it may become apparent that drinking in pubs is no longer quite in sympathy with the kind of life that he or she is leading as an orthodox Jew (or may not be, depending on the kind of pub, the kind of drinking and the kind of orthodoxy!). If it does become apparent that the convert's pub days are over, the resulting loss of companionship just has to be accepted as part of the natural ebb and flow of ones social relationships.

It may be worth mentioning briefly two other practical reasons why it may be impossible to maintain former friendships at the same level.

First, the convert may well find that the place in which they used to live does not provide the necessary facilities to support life as an orthodox Jew and that it is necessary to move. Even in London, where as already mentioned it is generally possible to buy a reasonable range of kosher food, that may not be enough. To have a synagogue within sufficiently easy reach to allow attendance twice a day (for men) is the difference between prayer being a luxury and a burden: and living in a vibrant and exciting atmosphere of orthodoxy (whether as part of a chareidi community or as part of a dati leumi community) is an essential for most people if they are not just to maintain standards of ritual observance but continually to grow spiritually. And once one has moved away from an area, it is likely to be difficult or impossible to maintain friendships to the same extent as when one was local.

Secondly, in the case of a young convert who is not married, it will no longer be possible to maintain a close friendship with a member of the other sex, Jewish or non-Jewish, at least without marrying him or her. This does not mean that the convert cannot keep in contact with unmarried friends of the other sex, but anything in the nature of a really close friendship is incompatible with orthodox life.

Finally on this aspect of the process, it may be worth noting that the tensions between a convert and his or her former friends may actually be greater in the case of Jewish friends than in the case of non-Jewish friends. During the conversion process the convert will go through the sometimes troubling experience of watching his or her Jewish friends "doing it all wrong". That may not be a problem for those friends who do not consider themselves observant Jews: but there are many who consider themselves orthodox and are yet appallingly ignorant of what orthodox Judaism actually involves. Many of those with whom a prospective convert comes into contact, and who may have played a part in introducing the convert to Jewish practice, find that they are rapidly left behind as the convert becomes knowledgeable in the intricacies of all manner of halachic areas the very existence of which was unknown to them. That inevitably causes tensions, and needs to be handled with sensitivity in very much the same way as the relationship with the convert's family. The change from trusted mentor to poor relation is difficult for both sides to handle.

Question 22 – Do I have to be a Zionist to become Jewish?

This is a terribly important question at this point in our history, when the State of Israel is under increasingly sharp criticism in respect both of the occupation of certain territories and also of general issues in the treatment of Arab citizens and others. Many human rights groups, for example, have Israel almost at the top of their international agendas.

One may suspect that in some cases there is a religious or anti-religious motive underneath the zeal with which Israel is criticised, and it is certainly possible to detect a lack of consistency in the treatment in the media, for example, of Israel and certain other states that are not renowned for their respect for human rights; but it would be clearly wrong to dismiss all anti-Zionist sentiment as a mere cloak for latent antisemitism. Whether or not some people use political criticism of Israel as a convenient way of sanitising and rendering acceptable what is intended as implicit criticism of Jews and Judaism, it is beyond question that some very reasonable people, entirely devoid of religious prejudice, are genuinely and intensely concerned by some of the practices and policies of the modern Israeli State.

So what does a person do if he or she has a religious commitment to Jewish practice sufficient to motivate conversion, but at the same time is deeply unhappy about becoming complicit, so to speak, in the politics of the State of Israel? Can one become (or be) Jewish without becoming responsible for, and an implicit supporter of, the State of Israel?

One could give a simple answer to the question: being Jewish is not the same as being Israeli and there is no reason why a British Jew should be treated by anyone anywhere in the world as being responsible in any degree for the actions of the Israeli people or government.

Although this is superficially satisfying, and has a good deal of hard logic to commend it, it masks a complexity that deserves further analysis.

The reality is that the bond between the land of Israel and the Jewish people is more than a matter of liturgical aspiration. The Jews have prayed three times a day over the last two thousand years for the re-establishment of the Jewish state in Israel; and the notion of the land of Israel and its special role in the world is absolutely central to the Jewish religion. But in a sense, that is only the start, and an unsatisfactorily theoretical start, to understanding the emotional connection that exists in practice between the vast majority of Jews and the land

and State of Israel. Most Jews in the United Kingdom have friends or family or both living in Israel, in many cases very close family and many friends. Many of us have friends or family, or at least friends of friends or friends of family, whose children are serving in the Israeli army. The result of all this is that the most patriotic British Jew is still likely to feel some kind of connection with Israel as an entity. An attack on Israel is likely to arouse the emotions of Jews living all around the world.

Where does a convert come into the picture on this? To put the question at its strongest, can one sensibly convert to Judaism while being a committed anti-Zionist?

The first point to note is that at all significant anti-Israel rallies and events a tiny number of apparently orthodox Jews are paraded to the media, repudiating Zionism and demanding the end of the State of Israel. By their appearances these Jews belong to an ultra-orthodox Chassidic branch of Judaism, and they style themselves Neturei Karta. The convert with reservations about Israel should avoid drawing any comfort or indeed conclusions from these deluded nutcases. The Neturei Karta are, as it happens, in origin a movement based on a respectable philosophy arising as a divergent branch of Satmar Chassidus; and there are a number of people in the Neturei Karta movement today whose philosophy, while extreme and highly controversial, is consistent and measured, and does not lead them to behave with insensitivity or to ally themselves with undesirables. As is usually the case, however, those who lead unobjectionable lives do not seek much in the way of a media presence, and are therefore largely unknown. The tiny number of black-coated Jews who habitually demonstrate with violent enemies of Israel, and notoriously attended a conference of Holocaust-denial in Iran, can be discounted as representatives of the Jewish community, and neither a prospective convert nor anyone else should be encouraged to think of their behaviour as acceptable in the eyes of all but an absolutely tiny number.

But that does not mean that on conversion a person is expected to become an uncritical supporter of Israel, or even a supporter of Israel as a political entity at all. It will be required of a convert that he or she subscribe to that part of our liturgy and belief that looks to the restoration of a Jewish state in the land of Israel, a state run according to the laws of the Torah in all their widest aspects. But that does not require approval of anything that is done at a secular political level. In particular, it does not require a convert to approve of anything that the State of Israel does in terms of military activity, the expansion of settlements, the continued occupation of land acquired in the course of defending the country against attack in the 1967 war, the civic treatment of Arab citizens, or any other similar matter.

In all these matters the convert is entirely entitled to his or her own opinion, which need not take account of anyone else's: however, the convert will be wise to remember that many Jews are likely to have an emotional bond to Israel, based on the presence of family and friends who live there, which makes them sensitive to criticism of the country. As so often, therefore, there is a distinction to be drawn between the right to hold an opinion and the wisdom of expressing it without thought for the (possibly irrational) sensitivities of those listening.

Question 23 – What most needs to be changed?

The preceding questions and answers will make it clear that there are a number of aspects of the conversion process and system that disturb me, to different degrees and for different reasons.

Fundamentally, the system of conversion in the United Kingdom seems to me serviceable and sound, and better for the long-term interests of the convert and his or her family than what happens in many places elsewhere. But there are a few aspects of the process and the way it is perceived that disturb me, and a few small changes to these aspects could have a very significant effect on overall perceptions and on individual cases.

As to the Jewish public's attitude to conversion, there are fundamental problems of bigotry and exclusiveness which require for their resolution nothing more than a little honest introspection: so they are unlikely ever to be resolved.

Here are my recommendations, each of which is fairly obviously based on the discussion in the preceding questions and answers. The recommendations refer expressly to the process as it operates presently in the United Kingdom;

but some or all of them will be equally applicable elsewhere.

Recommendation 1 – Money: A fund should be established to cover or contribute towards the tutorial fees, and to assist with other expenses, of prospective converts who cannot reasonably easily fund the entire process without help. The fund should be administered by the conversion registrar of the London Beth Din, and should be subject to a rough and ready means-testing system. The fund is unlikely to need to be very heavily endowed, since the calls on it should be modest in practice, although of enormous potential significance both for individuals who need it and for the general perception of the way the conversion process works. The money should be raised generally by soliciting donations but, in particular, professional tutors should be invited to donate a small percentage of their tutorial income – perhaps some or all of the tenth that they are anyway obliged to give to charitable causes – to the fund; and many converts who have completed the process would doubtless be delighted to contribute, perhaps after a year or two when they find themselves more established financially. The existence of the fund should be mentioned to all candidates at the point at which the Beth Din assign them a tutor. The fund would be limited to providing assistance with costs of the conversion process, and would therefore not risk attracting anyone into the conversion process purely in order to be able to access the fund.

Recommendation 2 – Courtesy and efficiency: The Beth Din should regularly review its administrative procedures with a view to ensuring that prospective candidates, even those whose enquiry is at a very early stage, encounter only prompt, efficient and courteous service. All staff should be reminded regularly and frequently of the importance of giving an amiable and helpful impression. In particular, it should be accepted that the sincerity of candidates is not to be tested by exposure to discourtesy or inefficiency; and the further a person has come along the process towards successful conversion, the more ready the Beth Din should be to accommodate their wishes and at least to consider their convenience as much as the convenience of the Dayonim: principally, this requires more flexibility in the offering of appointments at convenient times and at reasonably short notice. Feedback forms should be distributed regularly both to casual enquirers and to advanced cases, and they should be invited to give their views openly about the quality of service they have received: in particular, a few months after each completed conversion the candidate should be encouraged to complete a final appraisal form.

Recommendation 3 – Tutors: The Beth Din should maintain and publish a list of approved tutors. As now, they should generally assign candidates to tutors in the first instance, but the list should give details of the tutors' qualifications and interests and a few other personal details, so that a candidate can see whether anyone on the list particularly interests them or is likely to be particularly suitable for them. The list should also set out standard rates of the tutors' charges and should declare any relevant interests. There should be a standard feedback form which candidates should be required to fill in every six months, and at the end of the process, reporting on their experience with their tutor and stressing any particular strengths or perceived weaknesses.

Recommendation 4 – Living with a family: Moving in with a family is an essential part of the process of learning what it is really like to live an observant Jewish life, and it should be part of the programme for every prospective convert, with very few exceptions (the only obvious one being the case of an already married couple, particularly one with children, for whom it would simply be impractical). But care should be taken to ensure that the experience is always the positive one that it could and should be. Families should be chosen with the same care as tutors: mere enthusiasm alone should not be enough to qualify a family as a host family, particularly if there is a financial element to their enthusiasm. The fact that it is very hard to find families who are able and willing to host prospective candidates should not be a reason for using hosts who do not have the necessary knowledge to impart and the skills required for imparting it. It should, however, be a reason for publicising the need for suitable families to come forward and offer themselves as hosts, perhaps for relatively short periods: there is no reason why a candidate should not spend time with more than one family. Families some or all of whose children have left home, or are studying away from home, and who therefore have some space to spare and a certain amount more time and energy than those with small children, are of course particularly appropriate for this function, and Rabbis in the community should stress how important and valuable it is.

Recommendation 5 – After-sales service: In the same way that a convert is assigned a tutor and normally a host family before conversion, he or she should be assigned a support family after conversion to ease the social and religious path for the first few years. This should be an automatic part of the process so that nobody need feel that accepting it is a tacit admission of weakness or dependency. The support family should be based in a community where the new convert lives, and should be responsible for introducing the convert where he or she is not already well known, and generally for supplying some of the social and domestic needs that are so often able to be performed by a person's family. In particular, they should take an active interest in attempting to find an appropriate marriage partner or in helping the convert to find someone for themselves. The new convert should also be offered as a matter of routine regular meetings with the Dayonim for the first five years after conversion, as well as the opportunity to continue learning with the pre-conversion tutor. The mere offer of occasional assistance is not enough: the Dayonim should make it a priority to pursue the ger with vigour and satisfy themselves that their entry into the community is going as well as possible in every way.

Recommendation 6 – Community structure

Synagogue communities need to think much more about what is done to redress the actual and perceived social disadvantages of gerim and others who lack the support of a strong family. Making families accessible to singles through invitations for Shabbos meals is important, but it is only a beginning. Community events should be designed deliberately to enable gerim and others to mix with the rest of the community on terms of equality, not as guests to whom a favour is being done.

Recommendation 7 – Shiduchim

The Rabbis around the world can and should do more to redress the unhappy situation that has been allowed to develop where gerus is treated as a serious disadvantage in approaching shiduchim. Not only should the Rabbis speak out against any prejudice against gerim as marriage partners; but they should speak regularly and fervently in favour of making a family connection with anyone who has made this difficult and inspiring journey. More than that, however, the Rabbis should go further out of their way to show honour to gerim and the families of gerim in all the many different ways available to community Rabbis, making it clear that these marks of respect are because of and not in spite of their status. The bigotry and prejudice within much of the Jewish community is to ingrained to be countered by anything less than a concerted campaign by the Rabbis to replace it with a real understanding of the worth and value of gerim to our community.

Recommendation 8 – Publicity:

There is a significant lack of understanding among even the Jewish public about how and why the process of gerus works. Questions like the Israeli conversion the authenticity of which is doubted in the United Kingdom are simply not understood, and it is generally thought that the wicked Dayonim are for their own perverse pleasure punishing innocent converts by making them jump through new and unnecessary hoops. The public are not told that the Israeli Rabbinate might have been prepared to assume a person's sincerity based on their plan to live in an orthodox area of Jerusalem, a presumption that is rebutted by their moving away two weeks after the conversion and going to live in an area of the United Kingdom without an orthodox community. The publicity unit of the United Synagogue, the Chief Rabbi's Office or the Board of Deputies (or any combination) should assign a specialist worker to countering press stories that focus on the unfairness of the gerus process, particularly on cases with an international element.

Afterthought

Thank you for reading this book. If I have offended you by anything in it, please accept my apologies. If I have made you think about the process of gerus as it works today, I am delighted. If I have been helpful, I am even more delighted.

Comments will be very welcome: I may even produce another edition taking them into account. I can be contacted at dgreenberg@hotmail.co.uk.

With thanks and good wishes,

Daniel Greenberg

Printed in Great Britain
by Amazon